Becoming a G.I. God Imitator

Basic Training for the Soul

Michelle Bankson

PRESS

Dedication

I dedicate this book to my Lord and Savior Jesus Christ. I truly know that I was only the pen for the Holy Spirit who wrote this book through me. I give Him all the glory, honor, and praise for placing me into this ministry for such a time as this.

Acknowledgements

I want to thank my husband for helping me with everything at home and with the children during the seven months of writing this book. Joseph, my love and respect for you have blossomed even greater during these months. I know without your love and support this book would still only be a dream. Thank you for being such a wonderful Husband, Father, and my Best Friend.

I also want to thank my Pastors, Dan and Cindy Mundt for being such an encouragement to me. Your love for the Lord and keeping Him first in your life has been such an awesome example to my family and my ministry. I love you both and cherish our friendship.

To my parents, Mema, and Lori McClellan for reading my book and honestly critiquing and helping me proofread it. Without you, this book would be missing a lot of commas!

To my sisters, brother and church family, thank you all for being my greatest cheerleaders! I am so blessed to have the best of the best all in one family!

Table of Contents

Introduction

When you picked up this book were you thinking, "Becoming a God Imitator sounds interesting!" or "Who in the world is Michelle Bankson?" Well, let me start from the beginning on how this book even came to be. In 1997, God told me I was going to write a book and one of the chapters was going to be titled *Stop, Drop, and Pray....* I was so excited, and I told my husband what God had said to me. My husband was enthusiastic in his response, but I remember sitting down at the computer thinking, *I don't know how to write a book. What will I even say?* I never told anyone except my husband about the book in fear that maybe it wasn't God who planted in me the idea to write. I also feared that people would think I wasn't smart enough to write a book. I would be among great men and women of God and feel so inadequate and, at times, wonder if God could really do anything with me. So I just placed God's request on the shelf of my heart. I told the Lord, "I will type if You supply the words."

A few years went by and nothing really happened. Then, in 2003, the Lord said, "It's time to start the book." In the early part of that year, I had had a dream. In this dream, I was in our church with some other ladies. As my pastor's wife Cindy and I stood in the foyer, I saw four women come into the church. They were beautifully dressed from head to toe. They walked in with poise and confidence and you could actually see the love of the Lord in their eyes. I turned to Cindy and said, "Who's that?" Cindy looked at me and casually said, "That is Kay Arthur." Then the four ladies walked into the library of our church, and that was the end of the dream. I had only recently heard Kay Arthur's name at the Bible study I was attending. My group had just finished a Beth Moore study and, as we were discussing our next study, someone suggested a study by Kay Arthur. That was all I knew of Mrs. Arthur.

I didn't understand the dream and got even more confused and a little freaked out the following day. I had just sat down to take a break from laundry, making beds, emptying the dishwasher, and chasing my children, ages six, three, and two, around when I turned on the TV. James Robison was on and I heard him say, "I would like to introduce my guest for today. Welcome…Kay Arthur." My heart began to beat a little faster. Then I thought it was going to explode when the TV camera panned to Mrs. Arthur! The lady who was on my TV screen was exactly the same lady who had been in my dream!

I immediately called my husband and told him what had happened. We had no idea what God was trying to tell me. I was in so much shock from the dream and seeing Kay Author on TV that I honestly never even found out why she was on James Robison's program.

A few more months passed, and I heard of a few girls in our church who were going to attend the 2003 National Women's Conference hosted by Kay Arthur. I knew I had to attend that conference with those ladies! I asked my husband if I could go, and, without hesitation, he said yes. So off I went to Chattanooga, Tennessee! There were seven of us going together. I knew three of the girls, and the other four attended different churches in our area. I knew I was to be there for a reason.

On the first day, as we were getting ready to go from the hotel to the convention center, God started to speak to me! All seven of us women piled into one van, and, as we were about to leave the parking lot, one of the ladies said, "We should stop and pray!" So the driver, whom I didn't even know at the time, whipped the van into a parking spot. When she did, she yelled, "Okay, everyone! Stop, drop, and pray!"

I could not believe what I had heard! I had never heard anyone use that phrase before! My heart kicked into high gear again, but I didn't say anything since no one knew about my book. I had just started writing one month before this conference. So, we prayed and off to the conference we went.

During the announcements that morning, Kay Arthur let us know that on Saturday there would be a question and answer session. Anyone who had a question could fill out a form, and the panel members would answer, each as she felt led. Seated on the panel would be all of the guest speakers. So, during one of my breaks, I picked up one of the papers to ask the question that I believe had been keeping me from fulfilling God's plan. My question was, "I know that God has called me to write books and to start preaching, but I don't feel adequate enough to do the job. Have any of you felt this way?" I never went to Bible College, and I definitely am not a Bible scholar. I have been married for almost twelve years and we have three small children. I've always known that God was going to do something great through me. At times, I even thought my ministry was primarily to be an encourager for my husband who is in the ministry, but I knew that we both were called to further His kingdom. Well, I made a spelling mistake on the paper designated for questions, so I just folded it up and slipped it into my Bible.

Mrs. Arthur was scheduled to speak the first night of the conference. I couldn't wait to actually see and hear this lady. After she began speaking, it was only a few minutes later that my eyes filled up with tears as I listened to her. There might have been close to ten thousand ladies at that conference, but Friday night felt like a one-on-one between Mrs. Arthur and me. She was teaching out of 2 Corinthians 4 and 5. It was verse 1 that made me smile, because it says, "Therefore, since we have this ministry, as we have received mercy, we do not lose heart." That verse spoke so loudly to me! It was just as though God were confirming to me once again that He had called both my husband and me into the ministry, and that we walk in mercy so we do not lose heart. That verse was such confirmation to me that I wanted to stand up and do the dance of joy – but it still didn't stop my feelings of inadequacy.

Mrs. Arthur told the audience to look back to 2 Corinthians 3:5. She read, "Not that we are adequate in ourselves to consider anything as coming from ourselves." Then she actually said, "I know, Precious One, as I stand here and teach you that I am totally inadequate for the task in my own flesh and my own ability. But I know that my adequacy is of Jesus Christ. And if it weren't, I wouldn't stand here and try to do the ministry that God has called me to do. So our adequacy is from God and that is what you have to remember. You have to remember that you have a ministry, and your ministry is something that God enables you to do because your adequacy is not found here." She pointed to herself. "Your adequacy is found in God." She went on to say that the verse continues with, "....God, who also made us adequate as servants of the new covenant."

Oh how my heart filled with excitement at hearing those words again! Then I knew, without a shadow of a doubt, that God had called me to write this book. Those of you who are holding this book in the palm of your hands, know this: I did not supply these words, but my Father God, through me, has shared them all. After God spoke to me, gave me a dream, and then spoke to me again through Kay Arthur, I knew I was alive for such a time as this!

My prayer for you is that you will develop such an awesome passion for the Lord that no matter where you are in your life, whether good or bad, you will Stop, Drop, and Pray and give Him the glory, which He deserves. The Bible says, "Therefore, whether you eat or drink, or whatever you do, do all to the glory of God." (1 Corinthians 10:31). God has a plan for you, my friend, and it doesn't matter who you are or what you are doing; today is your day. Offer yourself to Him and let Him know that you are here to further His kingdom. Amen.

CHAPTER 1

It's All About Relationship

Have you ever wondered why some people can accept Jesus as their personal Lord and Savior one day and then walk away from Him the very next day? I often think about that and wonder how they can just go back to the way they were living. How do people walk into our churches, feel the presence of God, fall on their knees, ask Jesus to come into their hearts, and then backslide a week later? I don't like to think about the thousands of people, even many who are churchgoers, who think that just because they are good people they will go to heaven. Thousands have not changed from their old ways. Some have no idea that a person can have a personal relationship with God. It saddens me to know that there are so many who are deceived and could be on their way to hell. I know many people who *believe in* God but don't *know* God. They might have even been raised in church, but when they got out on their own, they thought life was more fun doing it their way. It boggles my mind when I see faithful churchgoers stop going to church and jump right into the world's ways of thinking. It crushes me even more when I see people who love the Lord but have not yet "fallen in love" with Him, where they actually make Him their first love, and then live a life that is pleasing to Him.

God has equipped us to make us complete, and He works in us to do His will. Hebrews 13:20-21 says, "Now may the God of peace who brought up our Lord Jesus from the dead, that great Shepherd of the sheep, through the blood of the everlasting covenant, make you complete in every good work to do His will, working in you what is well pleasing in His sight, through Jesus Christ, to whom be glory forever and ever. Amen."

The devil has come to steal, kill, and destroy, and he has deceived many. I truly believe, however, that our own spiritual laziness is also to blame. Proverbs 13:3 says, "The soul of a lazy man desires, and has nothing; but the soul of the diligent shall be made rich." God has placed a Book of Instructions right in our hands, but we have to turn off the television, hop off the recliner and actually *read* this Book of Life.

In the Amplified Bible, Matthew 6:33 says, "But seek (aim at and strive after) first of all His kingdom and His righteousness (His way of doing and being right), and then all these things taken together will be given you besides." Most people think that after asking Jesus into their hearts that is enough, but they miss out on the whole purpose of why they were even created. They battle through life, calling on God only when there is a desperate need that they want Him to fulfill. To some, He is a God of convenience and whatever sounds or looks good at the time. Our relationship with Him doesn't work that way! He doesn't want to be our acquaintance; He wants to be our best friend, our first love.

I had the opportunity to share with our youth at the church I attend. During my time of studying and praying about what it was that God wanted me to share, He so awesomely dropped one word into my mind. I was reading Romans 8:29 where Paul shares, "For whom He foreknew, He also predestined to be conformed to the image of His Son, that He might be the firstborn among the brethren." I knew I was supposed to share from that verse, but I didn't know how He wanted me to do it. So I got up from where I was and started doing what every mom does every day – laundry. As I walked into my laundry room, God whispered in my ear one word that has changed my thinking forever. The word was *authentic*. I have to admit that I got excited that day! I had a feeling of anticipation that would not go away. I knew what the word authentic meant, but I still wanted to look it up. So I typed it into my trusty

computer and out came "conforming to an original so as to repro-
duce essential features" (Merriam-Webster Online Dictionary,
2004). That is when I knew God was about to share some very basic
information with me that could change peoples' ways of thinking. I
had just read in Romans that God had predestined us to be
conformed to the image of His son. Then I understood that the word
He had spoken so sweetly to me meant conforming to an original.
You cannot get anymore original than Jesus!

What does it mean to be conformed to His image? The word
conform means "to form one's appearance, manners or to be similar" (Merriam-Webster Online Dictionary, 2004). So Romans 8:29
could actually read, "For whom He foreknew, He also predestined
to be similar, forming one's appearance of the image of Jesus."
Going to church and asking Jesus into your heart is a must and is
totally awesome, but conforming to the image of Jesus is literally
beyond words. If everyone who calls himself or herself a Christian
would actually be an authentic man or woman of God, this world
would not be in the mess that it is in.

To those of you who are reading this book, I am here to tell you
that it takes more than just going to church on Sunday morning to
live a godly life. I have heard so many times that it is so hard to be a
Christian. A man might have asked Jesus into his heart but his
lifestyle shows that he obviously has not sought after Him. Did that
man even know that he could have a personal relationship with the
Lord Jesus Christ? Every moment of every day, we have the chance
to live an authentic, Christ-like life. We also have the ability to walk
straight into the world's ways. So why is it that some grab hold of
Jesus, while others slip off on their first challenge? Do they just not
get it, or are we even teaching it to them?

There are so many people in the world who think that God
predestined them to just go to heaven. If that were the case, we
could just be held down during the water baptism until the bubbles
stopped, and we would have fulfilled God's plan for our lives! God
has so much more for us to fulfill, and He has a perfect plan for
each of us. He created you and me to live an authentic life, and it is
only through God that we can fulfill His purpose.

You might be saying, "So how can I be conformed into the

image of His Son? How can I live an authentic Christ-like life when I don't even know Him?" That is just it! It is all about relationship with Him and how He wants us to be like Him. First John 3:2 says, "Beloved, now we are children of God; and it has not yet been revealed what we shall be, but we know that when He is revealed, we shall be like Him, for we shall see Him as He is."

Let me give you an example of what He desires from us. On our wedding day, when my husband-to-be and I stood in the church, hand in hand, repeating our vows to one another, it was one of the greatest days of my life. I have to admit, our wedding was one of the most beautiful weddings I have ever attended! We got married a few days after Christmas, so the church was already decorated beautifully with red flowers, greenery, and lights. We added even more. It was beautiful and quite picturesque. I will never forget walking down the aisle, staring at this man to whom I was about to commit my life and love to forever. As I met Joe at the altar, and as my daddy kissed me goodbye and placed my hand into my handsome groom's hand, my husband-to-be sang me a love song. There was not one dry eye in the church. We gazed into each other's eyes, we served each other communion and repeated our vows to one another. Then Joe gently placed his hands on my face and kissed his bride! It truly was the happiest, most memorable, most romantic day of my life. After the wedding, we went to a plantation for our reception. It was beautifully breathtaking. There we ate, cut our wedding cake, danced, and kissed some more. It was wonderful! I hoped that these feelings I was experiencing inside would never go away! When the reception had come to a close and people stood outside and in the foyer to throw birdseed at us, there was one car waiting for the two of us. We ran through the crowd, jumped into our car, and off we went to start our married life together.

You might be thinking, "Why did she tell me all of that?" Well, let me have you think upon this for a moment. What if, after that wonderful wedding and reception, I had looked into my husband's eyes and said, "Joseph, from now on, every Saturday night I want you to meet me right here at this church. We can hold hands, sing to one another, repeat our vows, hug and kiss each other, and sit and talk all evening long." Then picture me running alone through the crowd, getting in the car, and driving off. Do you think that my husband and I would still be married today, twelve years later, if we had only met on Saturday nights? Absolutely not! When we ask Jesus to be our Lord and Savior, just meeting Him once a week won't cause our relationship to last either.

Although the Bible says He will never leave you or forsake you, it does not add that *we* will never leave or forsake Him. We need to be in *constant* communion with Him. It is all about relationship. Does that mean we have to quit our jobs and become nuns or monks to have that constant communication going on? No! But, just as a husband and wife have to keep dating one another, talking to each other, and hearing "I love you," so it is with the relationship that God wants with us. Many have gone to church and have asked Jesus into their hearts. They might have even sung songs to Him, had communion, and vowed that they would make Him Lord of their lives. Then, after that wonderful time together, they told Him to meet them back at the church next Sunday.

Oh, friends, if you are one of those people, please know that there is so much more God has for you. Being an authentic Christian is not a hard thing! It is an awesome journey of living a life filled with the presence of God. It is about being faithful to the One with whom we have spoken our vows. The word faithful means "remaining loyal and steadfast, true to the facts or the original" (Merriam-Webster Online Dictionary, 2004). I love how God works! He showed me that He predestined us to be made in the image of His Son. He showed me that we need to live an authentic life, conforming to the original, who is Jesus. Conforming means to form one's appearance and manners, or to be similar. And then, He tops it off with the word faithful, which is being true to the original!

In this relationship of authenticity with God, we experience such blessings and over-whelming feeling that God would never divorce us. He will never leave us when we mess up and feel like failures (Hebrews 13:5). He will never turn His back on us. He is faithful and true. He is the One who can be our Everything. Does that mean when we have decided to have a relationship with the Lord that everything is going to be perfect? No, it won't be, but there is an assurance we will have in knowing that we can call upon the Lord. The Bible tells us that we are going to have trials, and things like death and sin are inevitable. So if we are going to have to go through all those things, I want *my* relationship with God to be unshakable before those things even happen! Even through death, there is life, if you have that personal relationship with Him. Even after sinning, praise God, there is always forgiveness from the Merciful One.

You might be saying, "I do want a relationship with God, but I don't know how." Many, I am sure, are thinking that they have tried but have not felt that closeness with God. They may not know how to conform one's appearance or manners to be similar to the Original. Let me end this chapter with this thought. My six-year-old daughter, Shelby, looks exactly like my husband. She seems to have my mannerisms, however, which is sometimes very good and sweet and sometimes very, very bad. There have been times when I've heard her talk to her Barbie dolls and say things to them that I have said to her, and that always makes me smile. There have also been times when I've heard her correcting her Barbies in a loud and harsh manner, and I've gotten very upset with myself because it was me she was copying. Even down to the way she huffs and puffs, she sounds exactly like me when I've gotten upset with her. I love it when I see her with our son and she tries to mother him like I do. She talks softly and bubbly to him like I do, and she mimics my every move. There are times when I have music on in our house. Depending on the song, I will quite often raise up my hands and sing a song to the Lord. It does my heart good when I stand at our kitchen window and hear my daughter out on her swing set singing as loudly as she can to the Lord. She is what my husband says is a "mini me." But can you see why? Although she physically looks like my husband, she spends so much time with me that she actually becomes a little "mini me."

That is how God wants our relationship with Him to be. The Word says in Ephesians 5:1, *"Therefore be imitators of God as dear children"*(emphasis added). He wants us to spend so much time with Him that we will actually take to heart this word "Christian" that we use so flippantly. Christian means Christ-like. He wants us to become more and more like Him. He wants to look down upon us and see His Son's image shining right through our beautiful faces.

I love what the Amplified Bible says in 2 Corinthians 3:18, "And all of us, as with unveiled face, [because we] continued to behold [in the Word of God] as in a mirror the glory of the Lord, are constantly being transfigured into His very own image in ever increasing splendor and from one degree of glory to another, [for this comes] from the Lord [who is] the spirit." This is not something that we do all by ourselves. He is with us every step of the way. In Acts 17:28, it says that we should seek the Lord, "for in Him we live and move and have our being, as also some of your own poets have said, 'For we are also His offspring.'"

So how do we seek after the Lord and build a relationship with Him? Well, my friend, the best is yet to come.

Notes

CHAPTER 2

It's All in the Book

L et's look at how to build a relationship with God. If a person wants to become a doctor, then he has to study and study and study until he has memorized every book that his teachers give him. If he doesn't study, he will never know the correct information he will need to become a doctor. God has given us, as Christians, a book called the Bible to study and memorize so we will know how to become like Christ. God has given us the Bible to live by every day. When we live according to His Word, we will live a life that is unshakable.

Joshua 1:8 says, "This book of the Law shall not depart from your mouth, but you shall meditate in it day and night, that you may observe to do according to all that is written in it. For then you will make your way prosperous, and then you will have good success." That right there should make us want to jump up, rub the dust off our Bibles, and start reading. Everyone wants to succeed in life! Right here is a promise that by doing what the Word says, we will make our way prosperous and then have good success.

I can hear you right now saying, "But I don't understand the Bible; it is just a bunch of stories. How can I meditate on something that seems so complex at times?" Well, I am going to tell on myself for a moment to let you know that I thought those same thoughts. Although it seems like many years, it was only fourteen years ago that I moved to Florida to get out of some friendships that were not healthy for me. I moved in with my oldest sister and her husband. At the time, they had a two-year-old boy named Jordan. My brother-in-law was the youth pastor of an awesome church in Orlando, and it was good for me to be living with them because all we did was go to church! We were at the church Sunday mornings, Sunday nights, Wednesday nights, and the youth group on Thursday nights. You could say that I was getting filled up with the Word. I would hear these awesome men of God preach, and they would make the Bible seem so understandable. It was when I would be all by myself at home and I would open up the Bible that it just wasn't the same. I would read a chapter and then think, "What was it that I just read?" I struggled with reading my Bible for years. My little nephew, Jordan, got a birthday present that I thought I would really enjoy. You are probably going to laugh, but the gift was the animated Bible stories on video! I remember reading the book of Esther and then watching the animated cartoon of Esther on TV. It was as though the video brought it to life for me! Then I could read that story again and even get more out of it!

I know that probably doesn't sound very spiritual or mature for a young woman to do, but I was desperate to make the Bible come to life for me. I had been a Christian for years and had attended church for as long as I could remember, but every time I would read the Bible by myself, I felt like I was starting all over again. One day I started praying that the Lord would bring this Book to life for me. I would pray Psalm 119:18 over myself. It says, "Open my eyes, that I may see wondrous things from Your law." I would confess verses 105, "Your word is a lamp to my feet and a light to my path;" 130, "The entrance of Your words gives light, it gives understanding to the simple;" and 133, "Direct; my steps by Your word." I would read and read, and even when the reading seemed overwhelming to me, I would yell out, "Faith comes by hearing, and hearing by the Word of God!" (Hebrews 13:5).

The Bible is a Book that never gets old. God speaks to me every day, and it is something fresh and wonderful. It always accomplishes His purpose through every word I read. Isaiah 55:10 and 11 says that very thing so sweetly. I encourage you to read all of Isaiah

55, but 10 and 11 says, "For as the rain comes down, and the snow from heaven, And do not return there, But water the earth, and make it bring forth and bud, That it may give seed to the sower And bread to the eater. So shall My word be that goes forth from My mouth; it shall not return to Me void. But it shall accomplish what I please. And it shall prosper in the thing for which I sent it."

Oh, to every believer who is reading this book, I encourage you to get into the Word. If you are not in the Word, you will spiritually starve. What do I mean by spiritually starve? If you have asked Jesus into your heart and only stay a Sunday-morning Christian, then you will not be able to stand up to the devil's temptations to sin. It is imperative that you stay filled up with the Word of God so that you cannot be shaken.

Before Jesus had even started preaching and having the great multitudes of people follow Him, He went to Jordan to be baptized by John the Baptist. Let me tell you what happened when Satan tempted Jesus. Just after Jesus was baptized in water, the Holy Spirit guided Him into the wilderness to be tested and tried by the devil. There, in the wilderness, Jesus fasted and prayed for forty day and forty nights. Afterwards, He was hungry. Then Satan came to Him and said, "If you are the Son of God, command that these stones become bread." Jesus answered him saying, "It is written, 'Man shall not live by bread alone, but by every word that proceeds from the mouth of God.'"

That story is found in Matthew, the fourth chapter. Stop now and read that chapter so you can see for yourself. It says, "...every word that proceeds from the mouth of God;" you can find all of those words right in the Bible. Also in the Amplified Bible, 2 Timothy 3:16 says, "Every Scripture is God-breathed (given by His inspiration) and profitable for instruction, for reproof and conviction of sin, for correction of error and discipline in obedience, [and] for training in righteousness (in holy living in conformity to God's will in thought, purpose, and action). So that every man of God may be complete and proficient, well fitted and thoroughly equipped for every good work."

Reading the Bible is an awesome way to build a relationship with God. The more we read it, the stronger our faith will become, and we will become spiritually mature. Jesus fasted and prayed for forty days and nights. When the devil came, Jesus was prepared to go against him.

Colossians 2:6-7 talks about walking in mature faith. In the Amplified Bible it says, "As you have therefore received Christ, [even] Jesus the Lord, [so] walk (regulate your lives and conduct yourselves) in union with and conformity to Him. Have the roots [of your being] firmly and deeply planted [in Him, fixed and founded in Him], being continually built up in Him, becoming increasingly more confirmed and established in the faith, just as you were taught, and abounding and overflowing in it with thanksgiving." It says to have the roots [of your being] firmly and deeply planted [in Him, fixed and founded in Him]. The only way we can do that is by reading and knowing the Word of God. God loves us and wants to bless us.

I love how Psalm 1 shows the difference between the godly and the ungodly. It says, [1]"Blessed is the man who walks not in the counsel of the ungodly, nor stands in the path of sinners, nor sits in the seat of the scornful; [2] but his delight is in the law of the Lord, and in His law he meditates day and night. [3]He shall be like a tree planted by the rivers of water, that brings forth its fruit in its season, whose leaf also shall not wither; and whatever he does shall prosper. [4]The ungodly are not so, but are like the chaff which the wind drives away. [5]Therefore the ungodly shall not stand in the judgment, not sinners in the congregation of the righteous. [6]For the Lord knows the way of the righteous, but the way of the ungodly shall perish."

To those of you who do not know Jesus, ask Him into your heart now! To those of you who do know Him, keep your delight in the law of the Lord, and in His law, which is the Bible. Meditate on it day and night. Meditating day and night might seem a little hard to some, but don't make it harder than it sounds. My three-year-old Abigail loves Barney the dinosaur and we have many of his videotapes. I would sometimes put a Barney tape on in the morning and then would quickly go through my house and pick up. But then all day I would catch myself singing, "I love you, you love me, we're a happy family." I was allowing myself to meditate on the songs from my daughter's tapes instead of meditating on the Lord.

The first thing we all should do the moment we wake up in the morning is pray and read the Word. It doesn't have to be an hour-long session on your knees. But allow yourself to start your day off right. Then we can meditate on those Scriptures we read. I also keep praise and worship music on constantly in my house so I can't help but meditate on Him day and night.

I pray that you shall be like a tree planted by the rivers of water, that brings forth its fruit in its season, and whatever you do shall prosper. Jesus says in John 15:5, "I am the vine, you are the branches. He who abides in Me, and I in him, bears much fruit; for without Me you can do nothing." In verses 7-8, Jesus also says, "If you abide in Me and My words abide in you, you will ask what you desire, and it shall be done for you. By this My Father is glorified, that you bear much fruit; so you will be My disciples." Oh, He loves us so much, my friends. Grab hold of Him and let the zeal of God consume you. Amen.

Notes

CHAPTER 3

Examine Your Heart

Let's take a look at the Bible and see through the Word of God how we can "form one's appearance and mannerisms and be similar to His image." How can we become "mini me's" in the eyes of God so that when people see us, they see the image of His Son?

In this chapter, I would like to introduce to you two men of God...one I'm sure you have heard of and one whom you might have never met. I would like to point out that in John 15:16, the Lord says, "You did not choose Me, but I chose you and appointed you that you should go and bear fruit, and that your fruit should remain, that whatever you ask the Father in My name He may give you." Please do not think you have made too many mistakes or have sinned so badly that God will not love you. He does love you and He created you for such a time as this! He chose you and has appointed you to know and do His Word so that it will remain and abide in you.

The first man of God I would like to introduce you to is King David. Let's take a quick look at the life of David. You can read in 1 Samuel 16 how God chose David. Samuel was a prophet of God, and the Lord told Samuel "to go to Jesse, the Bethlehemite who was the grandson of Ruth and Boaz. For I have provided Myself a king among his sons." So Samuel obeyed the Lord and went to Bethlehem. Then the Lord told Samuel something that we really need to look at and not just glance over. He said, "Do not look at his appearance or at his physical stature, because I have refused him. For the Lord does not see as man sees; for man looks at the outward appearance, but the Lord looks at the heart" (1 Samuel 16:7).

Let's stop here for a moment and examine our hearts. I believe it is truly important for us to take care of our outward appearance, but my concern is that there are many who can put on a good front when it comes to issues of the heart. People can walk into churches or even be among friends and have all the right words to say, but they have disobedience and who knows what else in their hearts. Though they might think they are climbing the ladder of success, that ladder has an end; and it is leaning up against a wall of destruction.

Strive daily to live a life of holiness. The Bible says in Colossians 3:16-17, "Let the word of Christ dwell in you richly in all wisdom, teaching, and admonishing one another in psalms and hymns and spiritual songs, singing with grace in your hearts to the Lord. And whatever you do in word or deed, do all in the name of the Lord Jesus, giving thanks to God the Father through Him." I pray that we take those verses to heart and start living that kind of life today.

Now we all know that David was a mighty man and he loved God very much. When Samuel anointed David to be king, Saul was already king. Lets back up a little to 1 Samuel 13. What I want you to see is that God chose Saul to be king over His people, but his heart was full of disobedience and he was more concerned over his outer appearance. He did not obey the commands God gave him through Samuel. In 1 Samuel 13:13-14, Samuel says to Saul, "You have done foolishly. You have not kept the commandment of the Lord your God, which He commanded you. For now the Lord would have established your kingdom over Israel forever. But now your kingdom shall not continue. The Lord has sought for Himself a man after His own heart, and the Lord has commanded him to be commander over His people, because you have not kept what the Lord commanded you."

We have all struggled with disobedience. In 1 Samuel, we are given an example that even though God chose Saul to be king and gave him words and commands through the prophet Samuel, Saul still put on a good front and was more concerned with his outward appearance than his heart. Samuel then ended his last time with

Saul by saying in 1 Samuel 15:22-23, "Has the Lord as great a delight in burnt offerings and sacrifices as in obeying the voice of the Lord? Behold, to obey is better than sacrifice, and to hearken than the fat of rams. For rebellion is as the sin of witchcraft, and stubbornness is as idolatry and teraphim (household good luck images.) Because you have rejected the word of the Lord, He also has rejected you from being king." Ouch! The sad thing is that Saul knew what to do, but he chose to reject the word of the Lord.

That rejection still goes on today. How many times have we heard of great men of God who have rejected the word of the Lord over their lives and have lost everything due to sin? Some have become so power and money hungry that their hearts are not even an issue anymore. It amazes me that we have the Word right in our hands and hearts, but some have chosen to keep it only in their hands. That is why we must press on every day to know the Father even more than yesterday. Stay filled up with the Word and keep our prayer life continual.

What did David have that Saul didn't? He had a heart that loved the Lord more than anything. Everyone knows the story of David and Goliath, but let's take a look at 1 Samuel 17:28 to see the condition of David's eldest brother's heart. Why did God choose David instead of his other brothers? Keep in mind that David was only a youth, probably in his early teens. Jesse, David's father, asked him to take some grain and bread to his brothers and cheese to his commander. So David went to the Valley of Elah where his three oldest brothers had gone to follow Saul to the battle. David left his packages with the baggage keeper and ran straight to the army. While he was there, Goliath came forth and spoke. David heard him, but all the men of Israel fled from Goliath and were terrified. So the men of Israel said, "Have you seen this man who has come up? Surely he has come up to defy Israel; and it shall be that the man who kills him the king will enrich with great riches, will give him his daughter, and give his father's house exemption from taxes in Israel" (1 Samuel 17:25).

Now listen to what David says in verse 26. "What shall be done for the man who kills this Philistine and takes away the reproach from Israel? For who is this uncircumcised Philistine that he should defy the armies of the living God?" And the men told him, "Thus shall it be done for the man who kills him." In verse 28, Eliab, David's oldest brother, heard David speak and his anger was aroused against David. He said, "Why did you come down here? And with whom have you left those few sheep in the wilderness? I know your pride and the insolence of your heart, for you have come down to see the battle." Now could this be why Eliab's heart was not chosen by God? He had anger in his heart and might have even been a tad prideful.

David then turned his back toward his brother; the word got to Saul, and he sent for David. David soon killed Goliath; he always behaved wisely and his name became highly esteemed. He always sought the Lord before everything he did. Saul became very angry with David because he thought the people liked David better than Saul. Saul searched and searched for David trying to kill him, but Saul was never able to find him. However, David came upon Saul three times and had the chance to kill Saul each time. Each time that happened, Saul didn't even know David was there until David either cut his robe or took his spear and jug of water to prove he was right by him. God's hand of protection was on David because he was obedient. Was David perfect? Absolutely not! But he did love the Lord with his whole heart.

Read 1 and 2 Samuel. Read the Book of Psalms right along with it and see and listen how David always worshipped the Lord after all of his victories and sinful times. David's life was going wonderfully! God's hand of protection was upon David, and he had favor in the eyes of the Lord. Then there was that one night when David awoke from his bed and took a little stroll to the roof of his home. It was then that King David committed a few sins.

I will try to give you the condensed version from 2 Samuel 11. David saw Bathsheba bathing. He inquired about her and found out she was the wife of Uriah the Hittite. But still, he sent for her. They slept together, and she conceived a child. David thought he would fix it all by sinning even more. He tried to convince Bathsheba's husband to go to her and sleep with her so then it would look like it was his child. Uriah's men were in battle, and he would not go to his wife. So, David sent a letter to Joab and even had Uriah deliver it to him. The letter said, "Send Uriah in the forefront of the hottest battle, and retreat from him that he may be struck down and die" (2 Samuel 11:15). In other words, David had him murdered. Wow! What was David thinking?

It makes my heart hurt to look at the life of David. Up until this time, God had done awesome things in David's life. Then one little stroll to the roof of his home changed his life and his children's lives forever.

After Uriah was murdered, David brought Bathsheba to his house and she became his wife. She had a son, but the Bible says that what David had done displeased the Lord. The Lord sent Nathan to David to give him a word from the Lord.

> [7]He said, "I anointed you king over Israel, and I delivered you from the hand of Saul. [8]I gave you your master's house and your master's wives into your keeping, and gave you the house of Israel an Judah. And if that had been too little, I also would have given you much more! [9]Why have you despised the commandment of the Lord, to do evil in His sight? You have killed Uriah the Hittite with the sword; you have taken his wife to be your wife, and have killed him with the sword of the people of Ammon. [10]Now therefore, the sword shall never depart from your house, because you have despised Me, and have taken the wife of Uriah the Hittite to be your wife." [11]Then the Lord said, "Behold I will raise up adversity against you from your own house; and I will take your wives before your eyes and give them to your neighbor, and he shall lie with your wives in the sight of this sun."
>
> [14]He finished by adding, "However, because by this deed you have given great occasion to the enemies of the Lord to blaspheme, the child also who is born to you shall surely die."
>
> 2 Samuel 12:7-11,14

Now you would think that maybe David would get mad at God and give up because of such great sin. Look at Psalm 51, however, and see what David prayed. Then you will know he was not perfect, but he had a heart that loved the Lord more than anything. Psalm 51 says,

> [1]Have mercy upon me, O God, according to Your loving kindness; according to the multitude of Your tender mercies, blot out my transgressions. [2]Wash me thoroughly from my iniquity, and cleanse me from my sin.
>
> [3]For I acknowledge my transgressions, and my sin is always before me. [4]Against You, You only, have I sinned, and done this evil in Your sight. That you may be found just when You speak, and blameless when You judge. [5]Behold, I was brought forth in iniquity, and in sin my mother conceived me.
>
> [6]Behold, You desire truth in the inward parts, and in the hidden part You will make me to know wisdom.
>
> [7]Purge me with hyssop, and I shall be clean; wash me, and I shall be whiter than snow. [8]Make me hear joy and gladness, that the bones You have broken may rejoice. [9]Hide Your face from my sins, and blot out all my iniquities.
>
> [10]Create in me a clean heart, O God, and renew a steadfast spirit within me. [11]Do not cast me away from Your presence, and do not take Your Holy Spirit from me.
>
> [12]Restore to me the joy of Your salvation. And uphold me by Your generous Spirit. [13]Then I will teach transgressors Your ways, and sinners shall be converted to You. [14]Deliver me from the guilt of bloodshed, O God, the God of my salvation, and my tongue shall sing aloud of Your righteousness. [15]O Lord, open my lips, and my mouth shall show forth Your praise. [16]For you do not desire sacrifice, or else

I would give it; You do not delight in burnt offering. [17]The sacrifices of God are a broken spirit, a broken and a contrite heart. These, O God, You will not despise.

[18]Do good in Your good pleasure to Zion; build the walls of Jerusalem. [19]Then You shall be pleased with the sacrifices of righteousness, with burnt offering and whole burnt offering; Then they shall offer bulls on Your altar.

Oh beloved, this is where the Church sometimes misses it and just lets sin take over its life due to guilt. David messed up big time! In everything we do there are good consequences and bad consequences. You can start reading at 2 Samuel 13 to 1 Kings 2 and read all of the bad consequences that took place due to David's sin. David still chose to pray and repent and to be restored, however, so he could teach transgressors His ways, so sinners would be converted to the Lord. It even says in Psalms 89:3-4, which is a contemplation of Ethan the Ezrahite, "the Lord has made a covenant with My chosen, I have sworn to My servant David: your seed I will establish forever, and build up your throne to all generations." It also says a little further down in verse 27-29, "also I will make him My firstborn, the highest of the kings of the earth. My mercy I will keep for him forever, and My covenant shall stand firm with him. His seed also I will make to endure forever, and his throne as the days of heaven." That same covenant He has promised to us! Remember back in the first chapter I was talking about Romans 8:29, which says, "For whom He foreknew, He also predestined to be conformed to the image of His Son, that He might be the firstborn among many brethren." What does that mean? Well, keep reading! In verses 30-31, it says, "Moreover whom He predestined, these He also called: whom He called, these He also justified, and whom He justified, these He also glorified. What then shall we say to these things? If God is for us, who can be against us?"

Oh, how I pray this is ministering to you. Even though David had sinned and displeased the Lord, the Lord would not go back on His word. He had made a covenant with David, and just because

David messed up, God wouldn't leave him or squash him with His thumb. It's just like a married couple. They make a covenant with each other, so they stay together and make it work. But in today's world, there are so many who think even when they are walking down the aisle, "Well, if this doesn't work out or if he isn't the one, we will just split up and start all over." They have no idea what love is or what a covenant is. God is love, and He holds His covenant with us no matter what. I will say it again, "It's all about relationship!"

If it had not been for David, we would not have over half the book of Psalms. When you don't know what to pray, open up your Bible to the book of Psalms and pray psalms over your life. Psalms bring prayer and praise together as one. When you start speaking and singing them out, you are going to start seeing some awesome miracles take place in your life!

When King David died, his son Solomon became king. The Lord came and spoke to Solomon twice. The first time was in 1 Kings 3:5. God said, "Ask! What shall I give you?" Solomon asked for an understanding heart to judge His people and that he could discern between good and evil. So the Lord gave to him a wise and understanding heart, plus he got a bonus of riches and honor. Then the Lord ended what He was speaking to Solomon in verse 14 by adding, "So if you walk in My ways, to keep My statues and My commandments, as your father David walked, then I will lengthen your days." The second time the Lord spoke to Solomon was in 1 Kings 9:2-9. I want to show you a few of those verses to see how God felt about David. In verse 4, the Lord said, "Now if you walk before Me as your father David walked, in integrity of heart and in uprightness, to do according to all that I have commanded you, and if you keep My statues and My judgments." Notice here God did not bring up any of David's sins; He only spoke of David's heart and uprightness. That is what He is looking at in us—our hearts. We all are going to sin because we are not perfect. But, we all can walk in integrity of the heart and in uprightness.

You can read in first Kings that Solomon was a lover, not a fighter. The man had seven hundred wives who were princesses, and three hundred concubines. I can't even imagine that! Well, yes I can. I have read the Song of Solomon and that has to be better than any romance novel! But First Kings 11:4 is where Solomon blew it, where his father King David had not. It says, "For it was so, when Solomon was old, that his wives turned his heart after other gods; and his heart was not loyal to the Lord his God, as was the heart of his father David." Listen to what the Lord told Solomon about going after other gods. "Because you have done this, and have not kept My covenant and My statues, which I have commanded you, I will surely tear the kingdom away from you and give it to your servant. Nevertheless I will not do it in your days, for the sake of your father David; I will tear it out of the hand of your son. However I will not tear away the whole kingdom; I will give one tribe to your son for the sake of my servant David, and for the sake of Jerusalem which I have chosen."

Can you see the difference between David and Solomon? David loved the Lord with all his heart, and you can see through reading the book of Psalms that not even sin changed that. Solomon loved the Lord, but it seems he put his love for women above the love he had for God. As a result, he lost everything.

The first and greatest commandment is this: Jesus said, "You shall love the Lord your God with all your heart, with all your soul, and with all your mind" (Matthew 22:37). Dear Readers, it is time to get serious about your walk with the Lord. The more we give into our flesh and into the world's ways, the longer it is going to take us to feel fulfilled. Only our walk with the Lord can fulfill our lives. Your husband or your wife won't fulfill your life; money is not the answer. The only answer is having a passion and longing for the Lord Jesus Christ.

I remember when I started praying (and still do pray) that God would use me to further His kingdom, that I would know Him in a greater way, and that He would give me a heart that loves Him more than anything. My friends, it says in the Bible just to ask, so do it, and do it now! Pray aloud, *Father God, here I am. Create in me a clean heart. Pour your love upon me so that it overflows to every-one I come in contact with. Give me a heart that loves You and desires You more than anything. Use me, Father, to further Your kingdom, and let Your will be done in my life on earth as it is in heaven. Let Your Word become alive to me and help me walk out your commandments. For it is my reasonable service that I shall present myself, holy and acceptable to You. I love you, Jesus! Amen.*

The second man of God who I would like to introduce to you is my younger brother, Andrew. My mom had already had three little girls and thought her quiver was full; however, my oldest sister, who was nine at the time, didn't think so. She wanted a brother very badly, and she heard of how she could get one. We attended a church in Ft. Wayne, Indiana, called Blackhawk Baptist Church. Pastor David Jeremiah, who now pastors in California, was our pastor at the time. He taught my sister's Sunday school class one morning, and he taught on John 14. My sister grabbed hold of a verse he read and would not let go of it. Verse 14 was what caught Emily's heart. It reads, "If you ask anything in My name, I will do it." So my sister asked Jesus for a baby brother, and she knew she was going to get one. She went straight to my mom and dad after church and said, "Mommy, Daddy... guess what? We are going to have a baby brother!" My mom just smiled and patted her on the head and said, "We are? What makes you think so?" Emily said, "Well, Pastor Jeremiah said I could ask and Jesus would give me a brother."

For months Emily prayed and told all her friends and neighbors she was going to have a brother. She specifically and persistently prayed every day for a brother, and she believed that what she asked for she would receive. Several months had passed, and my mom was at Emily's school. As she was walking down the hall, someone tapped her on the shoulder. It was Emily's teacher, who whispered to my mom, "Congratulations!" My mom said, "For what?" The teacher replied, "Well, you're expecting, aren't you?" And Mom said, "No!" Emily's teacher said, "Well, Emily said you are."

It was just a few weeks later when my mom woke up feeling very sick. She told my dad that she was either dying or pregnant. Later on that afternoon they found out that she was not dying; and nine months later Andrew Thomas was born!

From the time of his birth until today, you can tell that God's hand of protection has always been on my brother. There are honestly too many stories of how God saved him from destruction or death to write in this one book. One story that stands out in my mind, however, was when he was about three and he opened the refrigerator door. Just as he did, Emily walked into the kitchen and pulled him back from the refrigerator. When he backed up, a glass container of cranberry juice fell out and shattered all over the floor. If Emily hadn't been there, he would have gotten knocked right in the head with that bottle of juice and could have been severely hurt. Another time, Andrew was out riding his big wheel in front of our house. My mom was on the phone watching him out the bay window. As he was on the sidewalk riding his big wheel, our neighbor was backing out of his garage and didn't see Andrew. All my mom could do was just pound on the window and yell, "Jesus save him!" Then she saw Andrew thrust forward, as if an angel had pushed him out of the way of the car. The neighbor across the street happened to see it all. When my mom and the neighbor came outside to hold Andrew, the neighbor said there had to have been an angel that pushed him past the car. Over and over again things like that happened to Andrew.

You might want to just stop, drop, and pray for your kids right now. It doesn't matter where they are. Pray for God's hand of protection upon them and plead the blood of Jesus over their lives.

When Andrew was in junior high and high school, he was very involved in golf and basketball. He was well liked and one of the popular kids. But Andrew had a heart for God, and loved Him more than anything. During an awards program for basketball, his coach presented Andrew with an award and shared a story of his. He said, "Andrew was not your typical high school student. He loved the Lord, and you can tell that by his actions. There was a time Andrew gave me a ride, and as I got in his car I noticed all the music cassettes that were in his car were Christian tapes. One was even on when the car started." My brother was never ashamed to let people know he was in love with the Lord Jesus Christ.

Was Andrew perfect and never in trouble? I will be the first to say, "No!" I remember visiting my parents in Florida when Andrew still lived at home. It was at a season of his life when he had put God on hold. I knew this to be true, because the boy talks in his sleep. My mom and dad had a little two-bedroom condo, and when all of the family would come for Christmas, most of us slept on the floor on air mattresses. I will never forget waking up in the night to hear my brother yell angrily and curse for about twenty seconds. I couldn't believe it! I had never heard him speak like that before. The awesome thing that happened, is that the next time we were all down to visit Andrew talked in his sleep again, but this time he said so sweetly, "It's okay, little one. God loves you and so do I." I believe God had that happen the second time just for me to know that Andrew was back on track. Before Andrew graduated from college, he was the youth pastor at his local church. Since then, he has married a wonderful woman of God, and they just had their first little miracle, Emily Grace. Andrew is now Executive Director for Youth for Christ in Highland County, Florida. He also preaches at numerous churches and youth camps. Andrew's lifestyle was walking with the fear of the Lord and choosing every-day to be a God Imitator.

I am sure that everyone who is reading this book has been on a diet at one point. Every diet I have ever heard of is mostly about having the right eating habits. It's a lifestyle. You have the choice every morning to wake up and eat a donut or have a bowl of fruit. It is the same way with our walk with Christ. It's a lifestyle of choosing to live a life of holiness or just live for yourself. We can choose to get fat and have no discipline in our lives, and then grow old and wonder why we even existed. Or, praise God, we can choose to live God-centered lives, walking in the fullness of Him. We can have assured success, for Psalm 1:3 says, "He shall be like a tree planted by the rivers of water, that brings forth its fruit in it season, whose leaf also shall not wither and whatever he does shall prosper." But the key is to do what Matthew 6:33 says, "Seek first the kingdom of God and His righteousness, and all these things shall be added to you." It says more than once in the Bible to love the Lord your God with all your heart, soul, and mind. Psalm 37:4 says, "Delight yourself also in the Lord, and He shall give you the desires of your heart."

Let me end this chapter with Romans 12:1-2. I ask that you make it your prayer every day to live this kind of life. *I beseech you therefore, brethren, by the mercies of God, that you present your bodies a living sacrifice, holy, acceptable to God, which is your reasonable service. And do not be conformed to this world, but be transformed by the renewing of your mind, that you may prove what is that good and acceptable and perfect will of God.*

Notes

CHAPTER FOUR

Basic Training

Do you believe that you are God's chosen one? It doesn't matter what you have done or what you have gone through, if you are a child of God, He has chosen you. You are the apple of His eye, and His love for you is more than you can even imagine!

In this chapter, we are going to go through Basic Training. When a person enlists in the service, the commanding officers do not immediately send him out to the battlefield with a gun wearing his street clothes. That would be crazy! That person would never make it out alive without the proper training. He would not have been able to develop the training and discipline that he needed to survive. Yet this happens all the time in our churches. You might have asked someone to come to church with you before, and maybe he or she "enlisted" into God's kingdom. A few weeks went by and he might have even come to church regularly. Then, all of a sudden, you didn't hear from him anymore. He ignored you and tried to keep a distance from you. Then you heard that last Friday night he was at the club drinking and partying like never before. What happened to that awesome Sunday morning when your friend knelt at the altar, crying and pouring his heart out to the Lord?

Can I give you my opinion? What happened was that he only enlisted and then skipped Basic Training. Everyone who asks Jesus to come into his or her heart needs some basic training to help keep his/her feet planted firmly so he/she can't be shaken.

Some things will have to change when we enlist into God's eternal kingdom. It could be just a few things for some, and it might be a whole bunch for others. When people enlist in the service, they bring the clothes on their backs and a few other necessities. Starting today my friend, all you need are the clothes on your back and the Word of God.

Here we go, men and women of God! Hop on the bus and let's go to basic training. In every kind of military service there is a chain of command. When we get off the bus we will meet the drill sergeant. The drill sergeant is the one who guides and trains us. Thank God, our drill sergeant will not take us off the bus and scream and yell at us. Our Drill Sergeant is the Holy Spirit, and it is the Holy Spirit who will cause us to walk like a man or woman of God. Ezekiel 36:27 says, "I will put My Spirit within you and cause you to walk in My statutes, and you will keep My judgments and do them."

When we get off the bus, we are no longer our own. We are God's! First Corinthians 6:19-20 says, "Do you not know that your body is the temple of the Holy Spirit who is in you, who you have from God, and you are not your own? For you were brought at a price; therefore glorify God in your body and in your spirit, which are God's."

All right, we have just arrived at basic training. Grab your Bible, and in an orderly fashion, step off the bus. Basic Training is not easy, friends. We might think we know how things get done, but in Basic Training we learn the *right* way to get it done. The first thing we will have to do is put on the Lord's clothes. They are called the Armor of God. Why do we need to put them on? The Bible says in Ephesians 6:11-12, "Put on the whole armor of God, that you may be able to stand against the wiles of the devil. For we do not wrestle against flesh and blood, but against principalities, against powers, against the rulers of the darkness of this age, against spiritual hosts of wickedness in the heavenly places." The armor of God is our fatigues and we need to keep it on at all times. Do you hear me? I can't hear you! Without the armor of God on, we would be like that person who enlisted into the service and then was sent out to battle in just the clothes on his back and a gun.

There are many new Christians as well as many Christians who have been saved for years who are trying so hard to live right, but they fail over and over again. I truly believe it is because they did not do what Ephesians 6:13 says to do: "Therefore take up the whole armor of God, that you may be able to withstand in the evil day, and having done all, to stand." Dear Reader, without putting on the armor of God and understanding who we are in Christ Jesus, we will not be able to stand. We have to start living a life pleasing to the Lord. That verse says to take up the whole armor of God. There are so many Christians who are only wearing the helmet of salvation. Ephesians 4:17-24 says,

> [17]This I say, therefore, and testify in the Lord, that you should no longer walk as the rest of the gentiles walk, in the futility of their mind, [18]having their understanding darkened, being alienated from the life of God, because of the ignorance that is in them, because of the blindness of their heart; [19]who, being past feeling, have given themselves over to lewdness, to work all uncleanness with greediness. [20]But you have not so learned Christ, [21]if indeed you have heard Him and have been taught by Him, as the truth is in Jesus: [22]that you put off, concerning your former conduct, the old man which grows corrupt according to the deceitful lust, [23]and be renewed in the spirit of your mind, [24]an that you put on the new man which was created according to God, in true righteousness and holiness.

So what does that mean? Well, I am going to tell on myself again to help show you what that means. When I was a senior in high school, my family moved from Indiana to North Carolina. We lived on the coast out on a little peninsula. The primary occupation in that area was fishing or clamming. To get to a grocery store or my high school, we had to travel between a half hour and forty-five minutes. In this area there was nothing for kids my age to do but get into trouble. Now when I left Indiana, I had some great Christian friends with whom to hang out. I was a typical "good girl" and had been a Christian since I could talk. I can honestly tell you I loved the Lord, but I was not *in love* with Him. Therefore, I didn't fear Him. I had my helmet of salvation on but was never fully dressed in my fatigues.

When we moved to North Carolina, just about everyone I knew drank and did drugs. I remember hanging out with a particular girl, and one day she wanted to go home to change her clothes. As we walked into her family's house she said, "Sorry it stinks in here. My mom and I have been smoking the bong all morning." I had no idea what a bong was until I walked into the family room, and there was her dad with this large, clear pipe—inhaling drugs! I couldn't believe what I was seeing. I grew up in a Christian home. Both my parents loved me and they loved the Lord. Honestly, I truly believed up until that point of my life that everyone was like my family.

During the next three to four months, I started drinking and doing drugs, going from one party to another. Now this was a really small town and my dad was an Executive Director at a retirement home for Merchant Marines. The word got to my parents one night that I had their Suburban with way too many people in it, and that I was too drunk to drive it. That night my parents met me at the front door of our home with tears in their eyes wondering, "What has happened to our youngest daughter?" For the next few weeks I was not allowed to go anywhere without one of my parents going with me.

Next thing I knew, my mom must have started some sort of a prayer chain because I started getting phone calls from people. My oldest sister would send me letters and cards telling me that she was praying that I would stop hanging out with these people and get my life back on track. I will never forget one day after work when I went to a friend's house and smoked some marijuana. As I was driving home, I honestly thought my shoulders were starting to enlarge. I would touch them and my finger would sink into my shoulders. I pulled over and stopped the car because I was starting to panic. I finally realized that it was just the shoulder pad in my shirt. It was then that I knew I needed to leave that little town in North Carolina before God's hand of protection would totally be lifted from me.

I went home. It just so happens that the pastor at the little church we were attending told my mom and dad that they needed to send me down to Florida to live with my sister and her husband. My brother-in-law was the youth pastor for Benny Hinn when he was pastor at Orlando Christian Center. The pastor thought that would be a good place for me to get focused. So I packed up my little Chevy Cavalier and headed to Orlando. It was then when I started living out Ephesians 4 and 5, and I no longer hung out with "the Gentiles," meaning those who did not have a personal relationship with Jesus. During the time I was walking with the Gentiles, I was also being alienated from God. The ignorance that was in them due to the blindness of their hearts obscured my mind from seeing God's truth. I had to put off my former conduct and be renewed in the spirit of my mind; and I put on the new man, created according to God in true righteousness and holiness. It was then that I became an imitator of God. Although I had once walked in darkness, I now am living in the light of the Lord and walking as a child of light. Daily I am finding out what is acceptable to the Lord. I have no fellowship with the unfruitful works of darkness but rather expose them. I am no longer being filled with alcohol, but rather I am being filled with the Spirit, speaking to others in psalms and hymns and spiritual songs, singing and making melody in my heart to the Lord. I am always giving thanks for all things to God my Father in the name of my Lord Jesus Christ. Glory hallelujah!

I have fallen in love with the Lord, I have put on my godly fatigues and I have been living for Jesus ever since. I am pursuing my Lord every day and will never stop chasing Him because I know that if I will draw near to Him, He will draw near to me. He truly is my first love! When I keep Him first in my life, everything else just falls into place because He gives me the desires of my heart. God is so good, and I pray that your passion in life is to pursue Him daily!

Do you remember the Gomer Pyle show? One of his famous lines was, "Well, golly!" Now he said it with his southern slur and would always swing his arm forward. I think this is a perfect time to swing your arm in front of you and say, "Well, golly!"

Okay, troops. This is what we will be taking to our barracks. Ephesians 6:14 says, "Stand therefore, having girded your waist with truth, having put on the breastplate of righteousness." "Girded" signifies a readiness for action, and before we are able to get into the action, we have to know the truth that we are God's righteousness. This truth is the first thing we need to take with us to our barracks. The second thing we need to take with us is found in Ephesians 6:15. It says, "and having shod your feet with the preparation of the gospel of peace." These are our combat boots, prepared and ready for us to wear as we go out and proclaim the gospel and to tell all that our God reigns! The third thing is found in verse 16, which says, "above all, taking the shield of faith with which you will be able to quench all the fiery darts of the wicked one." Do you want victory in your life? Then we need that shield of faith. First John 5:4 says, "For whatever is born of God overcomes the world. And this is the victory that has overcome the world- our faith." The last thing we will need is found in verse 17. It says, "And take the helmet of salvation and the sword of the Spirit, which is the word of God." We need to always guard our minds; never take our helmets off.

All right, my friend! We are now dressed and ready for battle. When we are fully dressed in the armor of God, we can go out on the battlefield and actually stand against the forces of hell. Now that we have all of our battle gear, go ahead and go to the barracks because it is time for lights out.

Honestly, I am crying so much right now that I can't type anymore. God is so good. These are not tears of sadness, but I am so thankful that God has said in Hebrews 13:5, "I will never leave you or forsake you." He truly is the Merciful One, and He loves you and me so much. My story might not have been as bad as yours, but God is a big God and He is waiting for you to give Him your all. Please know and understand that all we have to do is ask Jesus to forgive us of our sins and He will wipe our slate clean. Hebrews 8:12 says, "And I will forgive their wrongdoings, and *I will never again remember their sins.*" (emphasis added) Now meet me back here at 5:30 in the morning, fully dressed in the armor of God!

Okay troops, now that we know what we will be wearing every day, it is time to develop some discipline. I know you are probably saying, "Please, no...not discipline! I have the hardest time getting out of bed every morning and getting to work." Listen, we need discipline so we can disciple. John 15:7-8 says, "If you abide in Me, and My words abide in you, you will ask what you desire, and it shall be done for you. By this My father is glorified, that you bear much fruit; so you will be My disciples." If we are not disciplined enough to read, to study the Bible and to learn what God really thinks about us, how can we tell others about the awesomeness of God?

Let's start with some easy changes. First, let's talk about our mouths and what comes out of them. Psalm 19:14 says, "Let the words of my mouth and the meditation of my heart be acceptable in Your sight, O Lord, my strength and my Redeemer." Do you want to be pleasing to the Lord? Then it is time for us to "put some feet to our faith" and walk out Ephesians 4:25-32 (AMP). It says,

> 25Therefore, rejecting all falsity and being done now with it, let everyone express the truth with his neighbor, for we are all parts of one body and members one of another.
>
> 26When angry, do not sin; do not ever let your wrath (your exasperation, your fury or indignation) last until the sun goes down.
>
> 27Leave no [such] room or foothold for the devil [give no opportunity to him]. 28Let the thief steal no more, but rather let him be industrious, making an honest living with his own hands, so that he may be able to give to those in need.
>
> 29Let no foul or polluting language, nor evil word nor unwholesome or worthless talk [ever] come out of your mouth, but only speech as is good and beneficial to the spiritual progress of others, as is fitting to the need and the occasion, that it may be a blessing and give grace (God's favor) to those who hear it.
>
> 30And do not grieve the holy spirit of God [do not offend or vex or sadden Him], by Whom you were sealed (marked, branded as God's own, secured) for the day of redemption (of final deliverance through

Christ from evil and the consequences of sin).

[31]Let all bitterness and indignation and wrath (passion, rage, bad temper) and resentment (anger, animosity) and quarreling (brawling, clamor, contention) and slander (evil-speaking, abusive or blasphemous language) be banished from you, with all malice (spite, ill will, or baseness of any kind).

[32]And become useful and helpful and kind to one another, tenderhearted (compassionate, under-standing, loving-hearted), forgiving one another [readily and freely], as God in Christ forgave you.

Also in Ephesians 5:4 it says "Let there be no filthiness (obscenity, indecency) nor foolish and sinful (silly and corrupt) talk, nor coarse jesting, which are not fitting or becoming; but instead voice your thankfulness [to God] (AMP).

During this time of basic training, we must grab hold of what the Word of God says and just do it! If we want to be imitators of God, we will have to follow His example and walk in love at all times. I told you earlier that I have three children, and the way I am at church is exactly how I am at home. My children imitate what I say and do all the time. If I were to curse, yell, scream and get angry all the time, that is exactly what my children would start doing. Parents, if you get upset and curse in front of your children and then your child at some point gets upset and uses the same choice words you used, don't punish him. What you are doing in front of your children is saying to them that if mommy and daddy can talk this way, then so can they. Strive daily to be a godly exam-ple! People watch us even when we don't realize it. What we do and say can literally mean heaven or hell for some. If we are saved and attending church but still have mouth issues, let's start today and make a covenant with God that the words of our mouths and the meditation of our hearts will be acceptable to Him.

Another thing we need to look at during our time of Basic Training is church attendance. If you are not already attending a church, then it's time to start attending one. Now there are all kinds of churches out there, but you need to find a church that has a pastor who loves the Lord with all his heart and soul and strength. Ask God to send you to a church with a vision and one that truly cares about people, especially people who don't know Jesus. Meet with the pastor and find out in your time together if he is walking out *his* plan or the plan that *God* has given him. I only say that because there are so many people who go from church to church because they get offended at the pastor or they don't agree with everything he does, and then they stir up strife in the church. My friends, junk like that has to stop in the church! If my daughter wakes up grumpy and in a bad mood, my husband always says, "Shelby, are you going to have a good day?" He has trained Shelby to reply, "Yes, because I *choose* to have a good day." We need to ask ourselves that question every day and then reply yes, because I *choose* to.

Believe it or not, the devil does not care if we go to church. What he does care about is if we actually enter into the presence of God. He hates to see people supporting a pastor, actually loving him and praying for him even when they don't always agree with what he does. Do you really want to tick off the devil? Well, the next time the pastor or somebody in the church does something to make you mad or hurt your feelings, start praying blessings over that person. Please don't pray, "Oh, Lord, change them. Let them know they should be doing this or that, this way." That is not a prayer. That is manipulation and God will not honor it. Some people get so upset over the silliest things! If we are complaining because the pastor didn't say hello to us or the church used money to build or replace something and we don't approve, then we need to get over it! Think of it this way. Would you like it if the pastoral staff of your church came over to your house and asked to see your credit card statements and then actually had the nerve to question some of your purchases? No, you would not like that. You would actually be hurt and think that they didn't trust or love you. Let me show you in the Amplified Bible what we need to be doing. First Thessalonians 5:11-23 says,

> [11]Therefore encourage (admonish, exhort) one another and edify (strengthen and build up) one another, just as you are doing.

[12]Now also we beseech you, brethren, get to know those who labor among you [recognize them for what they are, acknowledge and appreciate and respect them all]-your leaders who are over you in the Lord and those who warn and kindly reprove and exhort you.

[13]And hold them in very high and most affectionate esteem in [intelligent and sympathetic] appreciation of their work. Be at peace among yourselves.

[14]And we earnestly beseech you, brethren, admonish (warn and seriously advise) those who are out of line [the loafers, the disorderly, and the unruly]; encourage the timid and fainthearted, help and give your support to the weak souls, [and] be very patient with everybody [always keeping your temper].

[15]See that none of you repays another with evil for evil, but always aim to show kindness and seek to do good to one another and to everybody.

[16]Be happy [in your faith] and rejoice and be glad-hearted continually (always). [17]Be unceasing in prayer [praying perseveringly];

[18]Thank God in everything [no matter what the circumstances may be, be thankful and give thanks], for this is the will of God for you [who are] in Christ Jesus [the Revealer and Mediator of that will].

[19]Do not quench (suppress or subdue) the [Holy] Spirit;

[20]do not spurn the gifts and utterances of the prophets [do not depreciate prophetic revelations nor despise inspired instruction or exhortation or warning.]

[21]But test and prove all things [until you can recognize] what is good; [to that] hold fast.

[22]Abstain from evil [shrink from it and keep aloof from it] in whatever form or whatever kind it

may be.

[23]And may the God of peace Himself sanctify you through and through [separate you from profane things, make you pure and wholly consecrated to God]; and may you spirit and soul and body be preserved sound and complete [and found] blameless at the coming of our Lord Jesus Christ (the Messiah).

Oh, how I pray that if you are feeling convicted right now on how you have treated your pastor or any of the leaders in your church, ask the Lord to forgive you and then start praying and bless the socks off of that man or woman of God. Do you want to grow and prosper in the Lord? Complaining and being easily offended will stop all blessings for us, Beloved. So, as part of our basic training, we must take up the cross and follow after Jesus. Please don't take up the cross and start crucifying your own church with it!

Attention! Okay, troops, how are you doing? Enlisting into the kingdom of God is so easy to do, but there will always be people questioning our faith and even trying to get us to fail. I have a cousin who married a Marine; he has been a Marine since 1985. On his second day of Officer Candidate School, he stood in line to get a haircut. They used to be called "Onion-heads." There were about eighty-five "officer candidates" in his platoon. They were all very tired and extremely exhausted because they were all up the night before doing various things.

Michael was near the end of the line and there was another candidate who was dressed in the same color clothes as Michael. They had not yet received their uniforms, so they were still in their civilian clothes. One of the drill sergeants saw this other guy talking in line and mistook him for Michael. The drill sergeant got up in Michael's face and questioned him several times about why he was talking in line. Each time Michael would tell the sergeant that he had not been talking, the sergeant would get increasingly more upset. Michael started feeling irritated that the sergeant would not believe him. Finally the sergeant said, "Drop and give me twenty." By this point Michael was so upset he stared right back at the sergeant and said, "With which arm?" Well, Michael really got his attention then, and he ended up doing push ups until the last officer candidate had received his haircut. What I want to point out here is that Michael stood firm in what he knew had happened. Even though the consequence meant doing one-handed push-ups in front of the barbershop in full view of his fellow Marines, then so be it.

Michael could have easily said, "This was the guy right here who was talking, so make this joker who isn't confessing do the push ups. But rather than stirring up more strife, he obeyed the drill sergeant, did his push-ups and it was over. He didn't pick a fight later on with the culprit who really was talking. They actually became great friends and are still friends to this day. Both of them recently served in Iraq. I am proud to say that Michael is a Lieutenant Colonel now and is still proudly serving in the Marines.

Stand firm in what you believe and choose to be the bigger person. Can I let you in on a little secret? We don't always *have* to be right. Find out what your purpose is and then try your best to live a life pleasing in His sight. I love what Psalms 119:1-6 says:

> [1]Blessed *are* the undefiled in the way, Who walk in the law of the Lord! [2]Blessed *are* those who keep His testimonies, Who seek Him with the whole heart! [3]They also do no iniquity; They walk in His ways. [4]You have commanded *us* To keep Your precepts diligently. [5]Oh, that my ways were directed To keep Your statutes! [6]Then I would not be ashamed, When I look into all Your commandments.

Desire after God and His example of living, and you will never be the same. Ask the Lord to teach you the ways of His statutes and to give you understanding of His Law. Then observe it with your whole heart and live out His commandments. Pray that God's mercies and loving-kindness would come upon you, so that you will always have an answer to those who taunt and reproach you.

Okay, troops! Attention! About face and repeat after me, "I have enlisted in the Kingdom of God. I shall keep His law continually forever and ever. I will walk at liberty, for I seek His precepts. I will speak of His testimonies also before Kings. I will not be ashamed. I will delight myself in His commandments, which I love. I will also lift up my hands to His commandments, which I love. And I will meditate on His statues."

As I end this chapter, let me leave you with this verse in Colossians 3:8-10. "But now put away and rid yourselves [completely] of all these things: anger, rage bad feelings toward others, curses and slander, and foulmouthed abuse and shameful utterances from your lips! [9]Do not lie to one another, for you have stripped off the old (unregenerate) self with its evil practices, [10]and have clothed yourselves with the new [spiritual self], [fuller and more perfect knowledge upon] knowledge after the image (the likeness) of Him Who created it" (AMP).

Notes

CHAPTER FIVE

Becoming a God Imitator

Becoming a God imitator might sound a little much, but I promise you that once you have read this chapter and put these steps into action, your life will never be the same! In this chapter I am going to show you the one person whom we should, as my daughter says, "Copy cat!" Ephesians 5:1 says, "Therefore be imitators of God as dear children." How do you become an imitator of God? You study His Word and the life of Jesus, and then you start doing what the Word says and what Jesus did.

We have to know God to become God imitators. The only way we can truly know Him is by reading and studying His Word, but it doesn't stop there. We can memorized the entire Bible, but that's not enough. We can't just be *hearers* of the Word—we have to be *doers* of the Word. James 1:22-24 says, "But be doers of the word, and not hearers only, deceiving yourselves. For if anyone is a hearer of the word and not a doer, he is like a man observing his natural face in a mirror. For he observes himself, goes away, and immediately forgets what kind of man he was." The Word of God says we are made in the image of Jesus, so when we look in mirrors, we should look at our reflections and see ourselves as being doers of the Word. Then we will see that we are looking at temples of God, knowing that the Spirit of God dwells in us. This is what I do not want you to miss! We have to *read* and *hear* the Word in order to *do* the Word. Knowing that we are the temples of God and that the Spirit of God dwells in us, we ought to be living glorious lives. So many people who know the Word look in their mirrors and still see spots and wrinkles, but those who know the Word and do what it commands ought to see more than conquerors, fruit of the Spirit, and bodies that are lined up with the Word of God.

There aren't enough pages in this book to share with you all the blessings God has for His children if they just live out His Word. We cannot be God imitators if we are not walking in love. Colossians 3 talks about putting on the new man who is renewed in knowledge according to the image of Him. The chapter talks about things we should *stop doing* like acting in anger, wrath, malice, blasphemy, and filthy language. Then it talks about things we *should* be doing like putting on tender mercies, kindness, humility, meekness, longsuffering, bearing with one another, and forgiving one another. The first thirteen verses of Chapter 3 pretty much list the dos and don'ts, but it is from verse 14 on that we must actually *start* doing.

> [14] But above all these things put on love, which is the bond of perfection. [15] And let the peace of God rule in your hearts, to which also you were called in one body; and be thankful. [16] Let the word of Christ dwell in you richly in all wisdom, teaching and admonishing one another in psalms and hymns and spiritual songs, singing with grace in your hearts to the Lord. [17] And *whatever* you do in word or deed, *do* all in the name of the Lord Jesus, giving thanks to God the Father through Him. [18] Wives, submit to your own husbands, as is fitting in the Lord. [19] Husbands, love your wives and do not be bitter toward them. [20] Children, obey your parents in all things, for this is well pleasing to the Lord. [21] Fathers, do not provoke your children, lest they become discouraged. [22] Bondservants, obey in all things your masters according to the flesh, not with eyeservice, as menpleasers, but in sincerity of heart, fearing God. [23] And

whatever you do, do it heartily, as to the Lord and not to men, [24] knowing that from the Lord you will receive the reward of the inheritance; for you serve the Lord Christ. [25] But he who does wrong will be repaid for what he has done, and there is no partiality.

I ask that you read these verses again and again, because the kind of life Paul is emphasizing here is "above all these things put on love." We already know that we are temples of God and that He dwells in us, but it is the constant battle against our own flesh that can move us straight into our old sinful natures. Knowing the kind of battle we must fight, it is imperative that we put on love because God *is* love. By meditating on that marvelous truth daily, we cannot help but succeed. First Corinthians 13 is so powerful when it speaks on love. I encourage you to stop now, read it and then examine your heart. Then take a look in the mirror and *know* just as you are known by God. If you think about it, everybody has an opinion about everyone else. You might be one of the greatest preachers and have great faith, but if you are envious, behave rudely, seek after your own desires, and/or parade yourself, then you are not abiding in love. Others might not know our hearts, but they know whether or not we walk in love. First Corinthians 12:31 says, "But earnestly desire the best gifts and yet I show you a more excellent way." The more excellent way is walking in love, because it is the greatest gift and it never fails.

The Bible says God is the Father of light; and when we asked Jesus into our hearts, we became light in the Lord. Therefore, Beloved, we are children of light walking in the fullness of our Creator! Therefore, live each day finding out what is acceptable to the Lord.

The Bible also says in 2 Peter 1:5-11, "But also for this very reason, giving all diligence, add to your faith virtue, to virtue knowledge, to knowledge self control, to self-control perseverance, to perseverance godliness to godliness brotherly kindness, and to brotherly kindness love. For if these things are yours and abound, you will be neither barren nor unfruitful in the knowledge of our Lord Jesus Christ. For he who lacks these things is shortsighted even to blindness, and has forgotten that he was cleansed from his old sins. Therefore, brethren be even more diligent to make your call and election sure, for if you do these things you will never stumble; for so an entrance will be supplied to you abundantly into the everlasting kingdom of our Lord and Savior Jesus Christ." Peter

knew the Word of God, and he was obviously teaching and admonishing fellow believers. He went on to say that he wanted to keep them stirred up, and I believe we need to keep doing the same thing today.

I attended a women's conference about two years ago. As I was at the altar pouring out my heart to God, a lady whom I didn't even know came up behind me to pray for me. God began speaking to her, and it was as though she were reading everything that I had on my heart. Then, she kept saying to me, "Keep it stirred up, honey, keep it stirred up." What she meant by that was we cannot get all on fire for God for a few days and then think we can grab hold of His coattails and be pulled through life. We have to be in constant communion with the Lord, staying fired up, and letting the zeal of God consume us daily. The Bible says in Ephesians 5:15-17, "See then that you walk circumspectly, not as fools but as wise, redeeming the time, because the days are evil. Therefore do not be unwise, but understand what the will of the Lord is." This next verse you might already know, but it should be my personal motto and your personal motto. If we are doers of this verse, then we will understand and know the perfect will of the Lord. Romans 12:1-2, "I beseech you therefore, Brethren, by the mercies of God that you present yourselves a living sacrifice, holy, and acceptable to God, which is your reasonable service. And do not be conformed to this world but be transformed by the renewing of your mind, that you may prove what is that good and acceptable and perfect will of God." By being doers of Romans 12:1 and 2, we will actually be proving that good and acceptable and perfect will of God!

You know, being a God imitator should excite you with such great joy! I just love the Word of God; at times, I feel like I cannot get enough of it. For me, being a Christian is all about living God's way because I love Him, I know His promises, and I stand on them.

So those are the first few steps toward being God imitators.

First, we have to *know* the Word and then be *doers* of the Word. We also must remember we are temples of God, and the Spirit of God dwells in us. We must always know that the promises of God are for us. Put on love daily, walk out Colossians 3 and present our bodies a living sacrifice to the Lord. I encourage you to love the Lord! If you love Him with your whole heart, soul, mind, and strength, you can't help but serve Him.

Let's take a look at the life of Jesus, the very one in whose image we were created. Here is a key issue. We are the Bride of Christ! If we truly believe that, we are going to want to know everything about our Groom. When you spend time with someone, you start picking up his or her mannerisms and become very similar to him or her. We can't just copy Jesus; we have to know and love Him.

The first thing you need to do if you haven't done it already is get baptized. This was the first thing Jesus did before His ministry began. "Why get baptized?" you might ask. When we ask Jesus to come into our hearts and ask Him to forgive us of our sins, then we become new creations in Christ. The Bible says that He will know us by the fruit of our labor. When you get baptized, as you are immersed in water, it is like you are at a burial and you are burying your old sinful man. As you rise up from the water, you are a new creation in Christ Jesus. The Bible says in Colossians "that you have died and your life is hidden with Christ in God. When Christ who is our life appears then you also will appear with Him in Glory." Just as Jesus was raised from the dead, we too, after we are baptized, should walk in the newness of life. After Jesus had been buried in the tomb for three days, He rose again. He then met His disciples in Galilee and they worshipped Him. Jesus then told them what His purpose was for them. That purpose is the same for us. Matthew 28:18-20 reveals it all: "And Jesus came and spoke to them saying, "All authority has been given to Me in heaven and on earth. Go therefore and make disciples of all the nations, baptizing them in the name of the Father and the Son and of the Holy Spirit. Teaching them to observe all things that I have commanded you; and lo, I am with you always, even to the end of the age."

If you know Jesus as your Savior and Lord, please let me encourage you to get baptized just like Jesus did. Learn to observe all things that God has commanded you, and always know that He will be with you.

Jesus said that we are the light of the world. We are a city that is set on a hill that cannot be hidden. He also tells us to let our light shine before men, that they may see our good works and glorify our Father in heaven. There are many who believe there is a God, and they might even believe there is a devil. What it comes down to, however, is that you must love the Lord with your whole heart, soul, mind, and strength. The Bible says in Matthew 7:21-23, "Not everyone who says to Me, Lord, Lord, shall enter the kingdom of heaven, but he who does the will of My father in heaven. Many will say to Me in that day, Lord, Lord, have we not prophesied in Your name, cast out demons in Your name, and done many wonders in Your name? And then I will declare to them I never knew you depart from Me, you who practice lawlessness!"

Jesus tells us very simply in Matthew 25 what we need to be doing every waking moment of every day. As you read the following passage, you decide for yourself if you are a goat or a sheep. He says when He comes in His glory with all the holy angels with Him that He will sit on the throne of His glory. It is then that all the nations will be gathered before Him, and it is there our Shepherd Jesus will separate His sheep from the goats. He will set the sheep on His right hand and the goats on His left. Then the King will say to His sheep, "Come, you blessed of My Father, inherit the kingdom prepared for you from the foundation of the world. For I was hungry and you gave me food; I was thirsty and you gave Me drink; I was a stranger and you took Me in; I was naked and you clothed Me; I was sick and you visited Me; I was in prison and you came to Me." In the Scriptures, even His sheep seemed a little confused at this point. They asked Him, "When did we do all of these things?" And here is the key! In verse 40 Jesus replies, "Assuredly I say to you, inasmuch as you did it to one of least of these My brethren, you did it to Me." Then he turned to the goats in verse 41 and said, "Depart from Me, you cursed into the everlasting fire prepared for the devil and his angels. For I was hungry and you gave Me no food; I was thirsty and you gave Me no drink; I was a stranger and you did not take me in, naked and you did not clothe Me, sick and in prison and you did not visit Me." Then the goats answered Jesus just like the sheep did, saying, "Lord, when did we see You hungry or thirsty or a stranger or naked or sick or in prison, and did not minister to You?" Then in verse 45 Jesus answered them, saying, "Assuredly, I say to you, inasmuch as you did not do it to one of the least of these, you did not do it to Me. And these will go away into everlasting punishment, but the righteous into eternal life."

Our ultimate fulfillment should be this, at stated in Luke 4:18-19: "The Spirit of the Lord is upon Me, because he has anointed Me to preach the gospel to the poor, He has sent Me to heal the Brokenhearted, to proclaim liberty to the captives and recovery of sight to the blind, to set at liberty those who are oppressed; to proclaim the acceptable year of the Lord." We should remind ourselves every day we get up out of our beds just why we are actually here. Some of you might already think you know why you are here because of the great job you have or the wonderful family you have, but God has placed you in those places so you can reach the world for Jesus. As I live each day, my desire and mission is that I will show or share the love of the Lord with everyone I meet. Does that mean I carry my Bible with me everywhere and quote John 3:16 in a deep religious voice? Absolutely not! It means waking up every morning, asking the Holy Spirit to direct my steps today, and being sensitive to His leading. Then I ask the Lord for divine appointments and give Him the glory for it all. Being like Jesus is neither a chore nor boring; it is exciting!

There are many ways to plant the seed of salvation into people's lives. One day my family and I made our famous butter cookies, and then we frosted them. We bought some decorative paper plates and took plates of cookies to all our surrounding neighbors. We said hello and told them we made the cookies for them to enjoy. It was a simple opening toward building a relationship and, at some point, sharing the gospel with them. Also, where we live there are many trees. During the fall, we constantly are raking the fallen leaves. My husband went out and bought a very powerful leaf blower to speed up the raking process. He liked his new toy so much he didn't just do our yard, but he also did four other houses on our street, which opened the door for him to talk with these people. There are many simple little things we can do and say to people that can have an effect on their lives in a huge way. Two of our neighbors are actually attending our church now! If we had never have spoken to them or just waved each time we saw them, we would have missed the opportunity big time.

There was a time when my husband and I took our two younger children to a home improvement store to buy some new doors for our house. We live in a very small town so we have to travel thirty minutes to get to this store. The kids had done great but were

getting a little tired and cranky while we were trying to check out, so I took them out to the truck and let my husband pay. As I walked up to our truck, there was a man sitting in his car in the next parking spot. He was listening to what I would consider hard rock music. As I was getting the kids into their car seats, God spoke to me and said, "There you go. Here is your divine appointment." Just then the man turned off his radio, as if he were waiting for me to speak to him. I got the kids in the car and I actually sat in the front seat for a minute wondering how God was going to do this. My husband came out with the doors we had purchased, and I got out to help him get them into the back of the truck. As I walked back to get in the cab I simply said to the man, "Isn't it a beautiful day out today?" He replied and we started to chitchat a little bit about the weather. Then I said to him, "Can I give you something to think about while you wait in your car?" He looked at me and nodded his head. I then said, "What do you think will happen to you

when you die?" He said, "Well, I probably will go to heaven or hell." At that point I was able to share with him for a few minutes about the purpose God has for him. I was able to encourage him to read his Bible and to get involved in a good local church. He told me that he had asked Jesus into his heart a long time ago but he only goes to church on special occasions. This is where people totally miss it! Just because we are good people or have even said, "Lord, Lord," it doesn't matter. If you have practiced lawlessness, then the Lord is going to tell you, "Depart from me."

What does that mean – lawlessness? Jesus said in Luke, "Can the blind lead the blind? Will they not both fall in the ditch? A disciple is not above his teacher, but everyone who is perfectly trained will be like his teacher" (Luke 6:39,40). Jesus was the teacher, and it wasn't until His disciples were perfectly trained by Him that they would also be like Him. We have that same training right in the Word of God. I love what my pastor says: "If you want to hear God speak to you in an audible voice, then read your Bible out loud, because it is the Word of God." By obeying the Word of God, you are also being perfectly trained. Practicing lawlessness and living the result of it is simply stated in Luke 6:49, "But he who heard and did nothing is like a man who built a house on the earth without a foundation, against which the stream beat vehemently and immediately it fell, And the ruin of that house was great." Jesus describes in Matthew the result of being perfectly trained by the Word: "Whoever hears these sayings of mine, and does them, I will liken him to a wise man who built his house on the rock." He also said in Luke 6:47-48, "Whoever comes to Me, and hears My sayings and does them, I will show you whom he is like. He is like a man building a house, who dug deep and laid the foundation on the rock. And when the flood arose, the stream beat vehemently against the house, and could not shake it, for it was founded on the rock."

By being God imitators, we are like that man who built his house on a foundation that could not be shaken. Did you get that? You are the house and your foundation is knowing and doing the Word of God. By knowing and doing the Word, you can stand firm and not be shaken when you feel like you are being beaten in every area. Do you even realize what blessings God has in store for you by being His imitator? To name just a few, you would be blessed coming in and going out, have wisdom, prosperity, health, the desires of your heart, fullness of joy, courage, strength, hope, fulfillment, favor, peace, and guidance. That should make you excited! Trust me, that is just a handful of the provisions He has for you!

Now let me ask you this. Was Jesus ever sad, upset, or in great pain? The answer to that is yes. His experience also means your life won't always be a great, blessed event. As a God imitator and a follower of Jesus, there will be times when you fall into various trials. In the first chapter of James, however, he said trials and difficulties perfectly train us to "count it all joy! Always know that the testing of our faith produces patience. But let patience have its perfect work that you may be perfect and complete, lacking nothing" (verses 2-4). Did Jesus ever lack anything He needed to do God's work? Never! But He did go through suffering and death for you so that you could become more like Him. He is so awesome and He loves you! All He is waiting for is for you to stand firm in who you are through Him. He created you for such a time as this, giving you a purpose and a destiny before you were even born. Call upon Him today, pray and intercede. Since your life is not your own, ask Him for your desires to be His desires and that you will fulfill everything He has planned for you. This brings me to the last chapter! I want to teach you how to pray to our heavenly Father. So get ready to stop, drop, and pray!

Notes

CHAPTER 6

Stop, Drop, and Pray

Do you take for granted the privilege of praying? I believe many believers take their relationship with God for granted. We seem to think praying to our heavenly Father is just like making a wish list for Christmas or birthday presents. Once I started spending more time with the Lord, my times of asking God for "things" stopped because His desires became my desires. The Bible says that He will give me the desires of my heart (Psalm 37:4). Therefore, I no longer have to ask for my desires; He gives them to me because I have delighted myself in Him! I have committed my ways to the Lord and have trusted in Him.

The Bible does say we are to ask. "Ask and it shall be given to you...."(Luke 11:9) It also says, "Ask anything in My name I will do it" (John 14:14) And, to give you one more, "Now this the confidence that we have in Him, that if we ask anything according to His will, he hears us. (1 John 5:14)

Back in the early' 90s, I worked for an apartment-locating service in Winter Park, Florida. People would call or come into the office, and we would help them locate an apartment in the area and price range they wanted. When I first started working there, I had to travel all over the Orlando area, visiting all the apartments we had contracted through us. I will never forget one morning when I stopped at an apartment complex I locked my keys in my car.. When

I shut my door, I realized my keys were still in the ignition and I prayed, "Lord, please help me!" Before I could even move away from my car, a policeman who lived there pulled in right beside my car, and within minutes my car was unlocked. I thanked God, went in for my tour of the complex and then left to visit the next one. The story doesn't stop there. I am almost embarrassed to say it, but –believe it or not – I did the exact same thing at the next apartment complex I visited! I shut and locked the door with no keys available to open it again. So, almost jokingly, I said, "Lord, I need help again." I walked into the office of the apartment complex and a policeman was standing at one of the desks. He walked out to my car, unlocked it, and I got my keys! I love it when God gives me "WOW moments"! I haven't even gotten to the good part of my story yet! The very next day I worked in our office. There were five of us who worked in this particular office; we were all Christians except one man named Scott. As I was getting my desk organized, Scott called in and said he would be a little late because he had locked his keys in his car at the gas station. When I heard what had happened, under my breath I prayed that God would do the same thing for Scott that He had done for me the day before. About a half hour later Scott walked into the office and one of the ladies said, "Wow! That was fast!" Scott had a huge smile on his face and replied, "You're not going to believe this, but just as I hung up the phone from calling the office, a policeman pulled into the parking lot and he was able to unlock my car." I thought that was so wonderful and wanted to stand up and do the dance of joy, but I kept cool. During a slow time in the office, I went over to Scott's desk and told him about what had happened to me the day before with my keys and my locked doors. I told him that I prayed for him that morning for God to do the same thing. I think he thought I was crazy, but I made him think a little bit. Later on that day, he started asking me all kinds of questions about the Bible and things that just did not make sense to him. God gave me a "WOW moment" and then used it for me to plant some seed into Scott's life. Beloved, please do not take prayer for granted; it is our privilege to pray to the Lord of Lords. Honestly, my friend, the first five chapters of this book are a must read before we can truly even understand the power of prayer. Prayer truly is all about our relationship with Jesus! We cannot become the Bride of Christ yet come and go as we wish. If you have asked Jesus to be your personal Lord and Savior, then you have made a covenant with Him and He with you. He isn't a God of convenience but rather a God who longs for us to fall in love with Him. He knew you before you were even born, and He has a plan and purpose for your life. God predestined you to become like Jesus, to be conformed to the image of His Son (Romans 8:29). You cannot just say, "I am a Christian," and then expect God to move in your life when you pray to Him. It is about being faithful to the One with whom you made a covenant. It is about learning who you are as you develop a deeper relationship with God. You are an Ambassador for Christ; when people see you, they should see the image of Jesus. If we truly walked out an authentic Christ-like life, we would know how to pray with the authority that God has given us!

To know and understand that authority, we must know the Word of God. Hebrews 4:12 says, "For the word of God is living and powerful, and sharper than any two-edged sword, piercing even to the division of soul and spirit, and joints and marrow, and is a discerner of the thoughts and intents of the heart." When I pray, I always have my Bible with me. Sometimes when I don't know what to pray, I open my Bible to the book of Psalms and start praying the Word of God over my life. I pace back and forth in my family room early in the morning and again when my kids are napping, and I pray aloud the Word of the Lord over my life. I encourage you to do so also! Meditate on the Word day and night. The more you know the Word, the easier it is to pray. I have been trying every week to memorize a chapter of the Bible. It has been life changing for me, and it has equipped me for every good work. By truly loving the Lord and knowing His Word, we can't help but have an effective prayer life.

I have many books written by Stormie Omartian. The prayers she has in her books are awesome because they all have Scriptures in them. I know that when I pray the prayers she has in her books, they are not just words—they are life because of the Word of God. We can't just read the Word; we need to live it. James 1:25 says, "But he who looks into the perfect law of liberty and continues in it, and is not forgetful hearer but a doer of the work, this one will be blessed in what he does." Jesus said in John 13:17, "If you know these things, blessed are you if you do them." When you are going through a trial in your life, I challenge you to look up all the verses in the Bible about that situation and start speaking the Word over it. The key to doing that is having faith. Without faith, we don't have anything. Hebrews 11 is a great chapter to read on faith. Verse 1 says, *"Now faith is the substance of things hoped for, the evidence of things not seen.* Verse 6 says, "But without faith it is impossible to please Him, for he who comes to God must believe that He is, and that He is a rewarder of those who diligently seek Him." The rest of the chapter gives examples of some of the great men and women of the Bible who had great faith. I encourage you to study these people and see what it is that you might be lacking. There are many who have faith and have sustained their faith but do not receive the tangible fulfillment of God's promises. Today, we have Jesus living in us so that we too can become great men and women of faith.

Many have great dreams that they want to fulfill in their lifetimes. So why is it that some people's dreams come to fruition and others' do not? It is because they didn't have great faith. It is very easy to put our eyes on man instead of God. When we trust in man we will get nowhere, but if we put our trust in Jesus, great things can happen! Some people live their lives going to church when it is convenient for them. The only time they open their Bibles is when they are at church, the pastor is preaching from a certain chapter and he tells the congregation to read along with him. They have allowed themselves to sway back and forth into the world's ways of thinking, always giving an explanation on why they can do or wear certain things. The Bible is very clear on what is right and wrong! The fact that times are changing does not allow Christians to compromise. The great heroes of the Bible had great faith because they did not compromise. I encourage you to study the book of Daniel and see how he would not compromise. Because of his faithfulness to the true and living God, he was blessed and used mightily. We all need to fear the Lord and earnestly strive to know Him more and more.

So what is our source of faith? It is the Bible. Romans 10:17 says, "Faith comes by hearing, and hearing by the Word of God." Do not ever think that reading your Bible is a waste of time, or that reading fifteen minutes a day is not really going to make a difference. Every time we pick up the Word of God and read it, we are building our faith. That is why the Bible says to meditate on the Word day and night. We will always be going from glory to glory! Hearing and doing the Word of God will fulfill the dreams that God has placed inside us. When I told my pastor about my dream of writing this book and preaching, he listened and encouraged me; but I will never forget for the rest of my life when he said to me, "Michelle, you are the only one who can stop your dream." Every time I feel like things are not going to work or who am I to write a book, I just remember what my pastor told me and move on.

Remember to always examine your heart before you pray. Every morning we should ask Jesus to reveal to us anything that is keeping us from going further with Him. How do you treat others? Do you always walk in love? When you do give in to sin, do you ask for forgiveness or do you keep dabbling in it? Are you worshiping only Jesus? I asked that last question because it is so easy to worship material things. In today's society, the television has deluged us with shows that talk about the rich and famous. It has programs that have young teenagers wearing close to nothing. I am outraged walking through my own town seeing young kids in outfits that even embarrass me. It is impossible to serve two Gods. The Bible clearly says in Exodus 34:14 that, "You shall worship no other god, for the Lord, whose name is Jealous, is a jealous God." We should all strive to live lives that are pleasing to the Lord. When we get dressed in the morning, ladies, we should ask the Lord, "Is this outfit appropriate for me to wear?"

We also need to guard our mouths. God has been teaching me that I don't have to talk as much as I do. For example, when I am spending time with a group of girls, I don't need to add my two cents worth into every conversation. Sometimes being an awesome friend to others is just listening to what they have to say and encouraging them instead of telling them what to do. It is important to live lives where we are always examining our hearts. We can ask the

Lord to reveal to us any hidden sins because Psalms 44:21 says, " God knows the secrets of our heart." It truly helps to walk in an attitude of praise. That means to try always to live our lives with the thought that "whatever I do today, Lord, I pray that it glorifies You."

If you haven't gone through basic training yet, then it is time to do so. It is time to stop *playing* church and start *being* the church. If you are not attending a church, please find one that is ALIVE and Bible-based. Then, when you find one, don't just go when you want, go every time the doors are opened! Ask God to show you where He wants you to serve in that church, and then go for it. Let me add to that saying that I don't believe God wants you to be in charge of more than one thing or be on every committee! When God tells you what to do, then put your time and energy into that one thing so you don't get burned out. Always remember that when you are put into a ministry position, you are working for the Lord. So whether you are a Sunday school teacher or cleaning the church, please know that God is pleased with your willingness.

Some of you who are reading this book have gone to church for years and still have not gone through basic training. How do you know if you have or haven't, you might be asking. That is an easy one. If you have asked Jesus into your heart but are still not living a life that is totally pleasing to Him, you need some basic training. If you have not totally understood the power and the love the Father has for you, then you need some basic training. You have to understand that the Spirit of the Lord is living in you and He is there to help guide you. Ezekiel 36:27 says, "I will put My Spirit within you and cause you to walk in My statues, and you will keep My judgments and do them." Your body is the temple of the Holy Spirit and the Bible says not to grieve the Holy Spirit.

How do we keep from grieving the Holy Spirit? I ask God every morning for wisdom for that day, because His Word says in James 1:5, "If any of you lacks wisdom, let him as of God, who gives to all liberally and without reproach, and it will be given to him." That doesn't mean that all of a sudden God is going to fill our heads with great solutions to the world's problems. Having wisdom is fearing the Lord. Job 28:28 says, "And to man He said, 'Behold, the fear of the Lord, that is wisdom, and to depart from evil is understanding.'"

Read and meditate on the book of Proverbs. It tells us both the dangers of ignoring wisdom and the rewards of seeking it.

I remember the first time I heard a preacher say that we should fear the Lord. I didn't understand; I thought he was telling all of us to be afraid of God. Fearing the Lord means to strive to obey Him. When we obey Him by actually doing what the Word of God says, then we are walking in wisdom. The Bible says over and over again to get wisdom and to get understanding. Proverbs 4 is a great chapter on which to meditate on and to memorize. It talks about not forgetting or turning away from wisdom. Wisdom is the principle thing. When we embrace wisdom, then wisdom will bring us honor and place on our heads ornaments of grace. Wisdom is the Word of God; it is our instruction book for life—not just a life to live but also a life to live that walks us through prosperity and success. Joshua 1:8 says that very thing, "This Book of the Law shall not depart from your mouth, but you shall meditate in it day and night, that you may observe to do according to all that is written in it. For then you will make your way prosperous, and then you will have good success." Glory to God! I love His Word! I totally agree with the Bible that you are a fool if you don't read it and live it out. Every promise of God is ours, but if we don't fear the Lord, we won't know how to receive those promises. I thank God for His Word! I absolutely love it! First Thessalonians 2:13 says, "For this reason we also thank God without ceasing, because when received the word of God which you heard from us, you welcomed it not as the word of men, but as it is in truth, the word of God, which also effectively works in you who believe."

By living out the Word of God, we are becoming God Imitators! When we pray, we are praying not with our might or power but by the Spirit of the Lord, according to Zechariah 4:6. Our prayer life becomes more than just a few minutes in the morning and at night; rather it turns into a constant communion with the Lord Jesus Christ. You know that when you pray, miracles happen and lives change. As God imitators, we start seeing the Bible come alive right before our eyes! We can speak forth the Word and call those things that are not to be. I like to read Ephesians 3:17-21 like this, "that Christ may dwell in **my** heart through faith; that **I** being rooted and grounded in love, may be able to comprehend with all the saints what is the width and length and depth and height- to know the love of Christ which passes knowledge; that **I** may be filled with the fullness of God. Now to Him who is able to do exceedingly abundantly above all that **I** ask or think, according to the power that works in **me**, to Him be glory in the church by Christ Jesus to all generations, forever and ever, Amen" (emphasis added). That is also a great prayer to pray when we are praying for someone else. Memorize the Word of God and then use the Word to pray. The Bible says in Proverbs 18:21, "Death and life are in the power of the tongue and those who love it will eat its fruit."

Back in 1994, I worked at a Credit Union in Apopka, Florida. I remember talking with some girls about babies and how expensive everything was, like diapers, wipes, and clothing. I jokingly said that I wanted to work at Wal-Mart when I got pregnant so I could buy all my diapers with a discount. In 1996, we moved to Indiana. We bought our first house, and I was pregnant with our first baby. I decided to get a job to bring in some extra money for the house, and guess where I got hired? I worked in the cash office for our local Wal-Mart. As I was sitting in the office one day counting money, God reminded me about what I had said two years ago. I stopped what I was doing and thought about it for a minute. The words that come out of our mouths truly do produce what we end up being. If you are always saying that you have no money, then you will never have money. If you always say that your life stinks, then don't think it is going to get any better. God taught me that day to guard my tongue and to always speak life into every situation.

As I end this book, let me encourage you just as Paul exhorted the Church. First Thessalonians 5:16-24 says, "Rejoice always, pray without ceasing, in everything give thanks; for this is the will of God in Christ Jesus for you. Do not quench the Spirit. Do not despise prophecies. Test all things; hold fast what is good. Abstain from every form of evil. Now may the God of peace Himself sanctify you completely; and may your whole spirit, soul, and body be preserved blameless at the coming of our Lord Jesus Christ. He who calls you is faithful, who also will do it." Strive every day to become a God imitator, and you will live a life that will stay centered in the will of God. I pray that you live long and prosper, just as your soul prospers, and that you find the truth, for the truth will make you free.

Notes

CHAPTER 7

Scriptures to Becoming a God Imitator

I am so proud of you for raising your standard and striving to become a God imitator. If you have asked Jesus to come into your life the Spirit of the living God dwells in you and has empowered you to live a Godly life. It is so important to read the Word of God and to have it in your mind and spirit in order to use it as a sword in time of need. I encourage you to read these scriptures every day let them become a part of you and see what God is going to do thru you. God bless you and your journey with Him.

> Therefore be imitators of God as dear children and walk in love as Christ also has loved us and given Himself for us, an offering and a sacrifice to God for a sweet-smelling aroma.
>
> Ephesians 5:1,2

> Assuredly, I say to you, unless you are converted and become as little children, you will be no means enter the kingdom of heaven. Therefore whoever humbles himself as this little child is the greatest in the kingdom of heaven.
>
> Matthew 18:3,4

But seek first the kingdom of God and his righteousness, and all these things shall be added to you.

Matthew 6:33

For whom He foreknew, he also predestined to be conformed to the image of His Son, that He might be the firstborn among many brethren. Moreover whom He predestined, these He also called; whom He called, these He also justified; and whom He justified, these He also glorified.

Romans 8:29,30

Now the Lord is the Spirit; and where the Spirit of the Lord is, there is liberty. But we all, with unveiled face, beholding as in a mirror the glory of the Lord, are being transformed into the same image from glory to glory just as by the spirit of the Lord.

2 Corinthians 3:17,18

For in Him we live and move and have our being, as also some of your own poets have said, 'For we are also His offspring.'

Acts 17:28

This Book of the Law shall not depart from your mouth, but you shall meditate in it day and night, that you may observe to do according to all that is written in it. For then you will make your way prosperous, and then you will have good success.

Joshua 1:8

Blessed are the undefiled in the way, who walk in the law of the Lord! Blessed are those who keep his testimonies, who seek Him with the whole heart! They also do no iniquity; they walk in His ways. You have commanded us to keep Your precepts diligently. Oh, that my ways were directed to keep Your statues! Then I would not be ashamed when I look into all Your commandments.

Psalm 119:1-6

Open my eyes, that I may see Wondrous things from Your law.

Psalm 119:18

Your word is a lamp to my feet and a light to my path.

Psalm 119:105

The entrance of your words gives light; it gives understanding to the simple. I opened my mouth and panted, for I long for Your commandments. Look upon me and be merciful to me, as Your custom is toward those who love Your name. Direct my steps by Your word, and let no iniquity have dominion over me.

Psalm 119:130-133

So then faith comes by hearing, and hearing by the word of God.

Romans 10:17

For as the rain comes down, and the snow from heaven and do not return there, but water the earth and make it bring forth and bud that it may give seed to the sower and bread to the eater. So shall My word be that goes forth from My mouth; It shall not return to me void, but it shall accomplish what I please and it shall prosper in the thing for which I sent it.

Isaiah 55:10,11

All Scripture is given by inspiration of God, and is profitable for doctrine for reproof, for correction, for instruction in righteousness, that the man of god may be complete, thoroughly equipped for every good work.

2Timothy 3:16,17

As you therefore have received Christ Jesus the Lord, so walk in Him, rooted and built up in Him and established in the faith, as you have been taught, abounding in it with thanksgiving.

Colossians 2:6,7

Blessed is the man who walks not in the counsel of the ungodly, nor stands in the path of sinner, nor sits in the seat of the scornful; but his delight is in the law of the Lord, and in His law he meditates day and night. He shall be like a tree planted by the rivers of water that brings forth its fruit in its season, whose leaf also shall not wither, and whatever he does shall prosper.

Psalm 1:1-3

I am the vine, you are the branches. He who abides in Me, and I in him, bears much fruit; for without Me you can do nothing. If anyone does not abide in Me, he is cast out as a branch and is withered; and they gather them and throw them into the fire, and they are burned. If you abide in me, and My words abide in you, you will ask what you desire, and it shall be done for you. By this My Father is glorified, that you bear much fruit; so you will be My disciples.

John 15:5-8

You did not choose Me, but I chose you and appointed you that you should go and bear fruit, and that your fruit should remain, that whatever you ask the Father in My name He may give you. These things I command you, that you love one another.

John 15:16,17

Therefore, as the elect of God, holy and beloved, put on tender mercies, kindness, humility, meekness, longsuffering; bearing with one another, and forgiving one another. If anyone has a complaint against another; even as Christ forgave you, so you also must do. But above all these things put on love, which is the bond of perfection.. And let the peace of God rule in your hearts, to which also you were called I one body; and be thankful. Let the word of Christ dwell in you richly in all wisdom, teaching and admonishing one another in psalms and hymns and spiritual songs, singing with grace in your hearts to the Lord. And whatever you do in word or deed, do all in the name of the Lord Jesus, giving thanks to God the Father through Him.

Colossians 3:12-17

Have mercy upon me, O God according to Your lovingkindness; according to the multitude of your tender mercies, blot out my transgressions. Wash me thoroughly from my iniquity and cleanse me from my sin.

For I acknowledge my transgressions, and my sin is always before me. Against You, You only, have I sinned, and done this evil in Your sight. That You may be found just when You speak, and blameless when You judge.

Behold, I was brought forth in iniquity, and in my sin my mother conceived me. Behold, You desire truth in the inward parts, and in the hidden part You will make me to know wisdom.

Purge me with hyssop, and I shall be clean; wash me, and I shall be whiter than snow. Make me hear joy and gladness, that the bones You have broken may rejoice. Hide your face from my sins and blot out all my iniquities.

Create in me a clean heart, O God, and renew a steadfast spirit within me. Do not cast me away from Your presence, and do not take Your Holt Spirit from me.

Restore to me the joy of Your salvation. And uphold me by Your generous Spirit. Then I will teach transgressors Your ways, and sinners shall be converted to You.

Deliver me from the guilt of bloodshed, O God, the God of my salvation, and my tongue shall sing aloud of Your righteousness. O Lord, open my lips and my mouth shall show forth Your praise. For you do not desire sacrifice, or else I would give it; You do not delight in burnt offering. The sacrifices of God are a broken spirit, a broken and contrite heart. These, O God, You will not despise.

Do good in your good pleasure to Zion; build the walls of Jerusalem. Then You shall be pleased with the sacrifices of righteousness, with burnt offering and whole burnt offering; then they shall offer bulls on Your altar.

Psalm 51

And I will forgive their wrongdoings, and I will never again remember their sins.

Hebrews 8:12

So if you walk in My ways, to keep My statutes and My commandments, as your father David walked, then I will lengthen your days.

1 Kings 3:14

I beseech you therefore, brethren, by the mercies of god, that you present your bodies a living sacrifice, holy, acceptable to God, which is your reasonable service. And do not be conformed to this world, but be transformed by the renewing of your mind, that you may prove what is that good and acceptable and perfect will of God.

Romans 12:1-2

I will put My Spirit within you and cause you to walk in My statues, and you will keep My judgments and do them.

Ezekiel 36:27

Do you not know that your body is the temple of the Holy Spirit who is in you, who you have from God, and you are not your own? For you were brought at a price; therefore glorify god in your body and in your spirit, what are God's.

1 Corinthians 6:19,20

Finally, my brethren, be strong in the Lord and in the power of His might. Put on the whole armor of god, that you may be able to stand against the wiles of the devil. For we do not wrestle against flesh and blood, but against principalities, against powers, against the ruler of the darkness of this age, against spiritual host of wickedness in the heavenly places. Therefore take up the whole armor of God, that you may be able to withstand in the evil day, and having done all, to stand.

Stand therefore, having girded your waist with truth, having put on the breastplate of righteousness, and having shod your feet with the preparation of the gospel of peace; above all, taking the shield of faith with which you will be able to quench all the fiery darts of the wicked one. And take the helmet of salvation and the sword of the spirit, which is the word of God; praying always with all prayers and supplication in the Spirit, being watchful to this end with all perseverance and supplication for all saints and for me, that utterance may be given to me, that I may open my mouth boldly to make known the mystery of the gospel, for which I am an ambassador in chains; that in it I may speak boldly, as I ought to speak.

Ephesians 6:10-20

Let the words of my mouth and the mediation of my heart be acceptable in Your sight, O Lord, my strength and my Redeemer.

Psalm 19:14

But now you yourselves are to put off all these: anger, wrath, malice, blasphemy, filthy language out of your mouth. Do not lie to one another, since you have put off the old man with his deed, and have put on the new man who is renewed in knowledge according to the image of Him who created him.

Colossians 3:8-10

But be doers of the word, and not hearers only, deceiving yourselves. For if anyone is a hearer of the word and not a doer, he is like a man observing his natural face in a mirror. For he observes himself, goes away, and immediately forgets what kind of man he was. But he who looks into the perfect law of liberty and continues in it, and is not forgetful hearer but a doer of the work, this one will be blessed in what he does.

James 1:22-25

See then that you walk circumspectly, not as fools but as wise, redeeming the time, because the days are evil. Therefore do not be unwise, but understand what the will of the Lord is.

Ephesians 5:15-17

Rejoice always, pray without ceasing, in everything give thanks; for this is the will of God in Christ Jesus for you. Do not quench the Spirit. Do not despise prophecies. Test all things; hold fast what is good. Abstain from every form of evil. Now may the God peace Himself sanctify you completely; and may your whole spirit, soul, and body be preserved blameless at the coming of our Lord Jesus Christ. He who calls you is faithful, who also will do it.

1 Thessalonians 5:16-24

And Jesus came and spoke to them saying, "All authority has been given to Me in heaven and on earth. Go therefore and make disciples of all the nations, baptizing them in the name of the Father and the Son and of the Holy Spirit. Teaching them to observe all things that I have commanded you; and lo, I am with you always, even to the end of the age."

Matthew 28:18-20

The Spirit of the Lord is upon Me, because He has anointed Me to preach the gospel to the poor, he has sent Me to heal the Brokenhearted, to proclaim liberty to the captives and recovery of sight to the blind, to set at liberty those who are oppressed; to proclaim the acceptable year of the Lord.

Luke 4:18,19

Whoever comes to Me, and hears My sayings and does them, I will show you whom he is like. He is like a man building a house, who dug deep and laid the foundation on the rock. And when the flood arose, the stream beat vehemently against the house, and could not shake it, for it was founded on the rock.

Luke 6:47,48

For the word of God is living and powerful, and sharper than any two-edged sword, piercing even to the division of soul and spirit, and joints and marrow, and is discerner of the thoughts and intents of the heart.

Hebrews 4:12

If you know these things, blessed are you if you do them.

John 13:17

Now faith is the substance of things hoped for, the evidence of things not seen.

Hebrews 11:1

But without faith it is impossible to please Him, for he who comes to God must believe that He is, and that He is a rewarder of those who diligently seek Him.

Hebrews 11:6

You shall worship no other god, for the Lord, whose name is Jealous, is a jealous God.

Exodus 34:14

If any of you lacks wisdom, let him ask of God, who gives to all liberally and without reproach, and it will be given to him.

James 1:5

Fear not, for I am with you; Be not dismayed, for I am your God. I will strengthen you, yes, I will help you, I will uphold you with My righteous right hand

Isaiah 41:10

Or do you not know that your body is the temple of the Holy Spirit *who is* in you, whom you have from God, and you are not your own? For you were bought at a price; therefore glorify God in your body and in your spirit, which are God's.

1 Corinthians 6:19,20

Jesus said to him, "I am the way, the truth, and the life. No one comes to the Father except through Me".

John 14:6

And you shall know the truth, and the truth shall make you free.

John 8:32

Finally, brethren, whatever things are true, whatever things *are* noble, whatever things *are* just, whatever things *are* pure, whatever things *are* lovely, whatever things *are* of good report, if *there is* any virtue and if *there is* anything praiseworthy—meditate on these things.

Philippians 4:8

I have been crucified with Christ; it is no longer I who live, but Christ lives in me; and the *life* which I now live in the flesh I live by faith in the Son of God, who loved me and gave Himself for me.

Galatians 2:20

I can do all things through Christ who strengthens me.

Philippians 4:13

The fear of the Lord *is* the beginning of wisdom; A good understanding have all those who do *His commandments.* His praise endures forever.

Psalm 111:10

If any of you lacks wisdom, let him ask of God, who gives to all liberally and without reproach, and it will be given to him.

James 1:5

Let the words of my mouth and the meditation of my heart Be acceptable in Your sight, O Lord, my strength and my Redeemer.

Psalm 19:14

Teach me Your way, O Lord; I will walk in Your truth; Unite my heart to fear Your name. I will praise You, O Lord my God, with all my heart, And I will glorify Your name forevermore.

Psalm 86:11,12

Fear not, for I *am* with you; Be not dismayed, for I *am* your God. I will strengthen you, Yes, I will help you, I will uphold you with My righteous right hand.'

Isaiah 41:10

So he answered and said to me: "This *is* the word of the Lord to Zerubbabel: 'Not by might nor by power, but by My Spirit,' Says the Lord of hosts.

Zechariah 4:6

The thief does not come except to steal, and to kill, and to destroy. I have come that they may have life, and that they may have *it* more abundantly.

John 10:10

Now may the God of hope fill you with all joy and peace in believing, that you may abound in hope by the power of the Holy Spirit.

Romans 15:13

For I am not ashamed of the gospel of Christ, for it is the power of God to salvation for everyone who believes, for the Jew first and also for the Greek.

Romans 1:16

Additional Notes

Notes

Notes

Contact Information

Living Gods Way Ministries
Michelle Bankson
527 Fulton Avenue
Rochester, Indiana 46975
1-877-875-4927
LivingGodsWay@godimitator.com
www.godimitator.com

Speaks in churches, conferences, seminars. Please contact if you are interested in booking her for your church or event.